SUSTAINING STRATEGIC READERS

Techniques for Supporting Content Literacy in Grades 6–12

VALERIE ELLERY
JENNIFER L. ROSENBOOM

INTERNATIONAL
Reading Association
800 Barksdale Road, PO Box 8139
Newark, DE 19714-8139, USA
www.reading.org

The International Reading Association attempts, through its publications, to provide a forum for a wide spectrum of opinions on reading. This policy permits divergent viewpoints without implying the endorsement of the Association.

Executive Editor, Publications   Shannon Fortner

Managing Editor   Christina M. Terranova

Editorial Associate   Wendy Logan

Design and Composition Manager   Anette Schuetz

Design and Composition Associate   Lisa Kochel

Art   Cover Design: Brad Tillinghast; Photography: © iStockphoto.com/Ekaterina Monakhova (cover far left), Jill Cushing (all other cover images; pp. 22, 48, 77, 111, bottom center), Angela Rosenboom (pp. 111, top left, top right)

Copyright 2011 by the International Reading Association, Inc.

The publisher would appreciate notification where errors occur so that they may be corrected in subsequent printings and/or editions.

Library of Congress Cataloging-in-Publication Data
Ellery, Valerie, 1964-
  Sustaining strategic readers : techniques for supporting content literacy in grades 6-12 / Valerie Ellery and Jennifer L. Rosenboom.
     p. cm.
  Includes bibliographical references and index.
  ISBN 978-0-87207-839-0
  1. Content area reading. 2. Language arts (Middle school) 3. Language arts (Secondary) I. Rosenboom, Jennifer L., 1955- II. Title.
  LB1050.455.E55 2011
  428.4071'2--dc22
                                                                2011003020

Suggested APA Reference
Ellery, V. & Rosenboom, J.L. (2011). *Sustaining strategic readers: Techniques for supporting content literacy in grades 6–12*. Newark, DE: International Reading Association.

In loving memory of my father, Lowell Oakley, who always taught me to identify my passion and make a difference.
—Jennifer

To my son, Nicholas, who persevered through the challenges of literacy learning and now has a legacy of love for learning.
—Valerie

Contents

About the Authors

Valerie Ellery has dedicated more than two decades to the field of literacy in various roles as a National Board Certified Teacher, curriculum specialist, mentor, reading coach, international consultant, and author. More than 20 years ago while teaching, she realized that her oldest son, Nick, had a reading problem. This personal experience launched her journey in the quest for understanding, What do proficient readers do?

After acquiring her master's degree in reading K–12 at the University of South Florida, Sarasota, Florida, United States, Valerie became a district curriculum specialist. This new role gave her the opportunity to model reading strategies, mentor teachers, and construct a road map for creating strategic readers. In 2005, her first book, *Creating Strategic Readers: Techniques for Developing Competency in Phonemic Awareness, Phonics, Fluency, Vocabulary, and Comprehension,* was published by the International Reading Association (IRA). The second edition was published in 2009. The book has been used internationally in universities as an undergraduate course, helping to propel the reading process to the forefront of education. Educators have shared that the techniques in the book are clear and concise and easy to implement in their classrooms.

In 2008, Valerie published a staff development DVD/VHS series titled *Creating Strategic Readers: Teaching Techniques for the Primary and Intermediate Grades* based on her first book. She is a coauthor of the 2009 Professional Development Facilitator's Guide to Farstrup and Samuels's (2002) *What Research Has to Say About Reading Instruction* (third edition), published by IRA. Currently, Valerie is an internationally known reading consultant who offers innovative, interactive, and motivating techniques with relevant and practical application. She is truly passionate about creating strategic readers.

Valerie carries that same passion into her home in Bradenton, Florida. She is a devoted wife to Gregg; mother to Nick, Derek, Jacey, and Brooke; grandmother; and a women's ministry leader to thousands. She has also published a book to empower women, titled *Equipping the Warrior Woman: Strategies to Awaken Your Purpose, Strength, and Confidence.*

The journey that started with Valerie's oldest son continues today. Nick, who overcame his reading difficulties, graduated with a biomedical degree from the U.S. Navy and is currently working in a hospital in Naples, Italy. He, along with his wife, Virginia, is continuing the legacy of strategic reading through his daughter, Evelyn Marie.

Author Information for Correspondence and Workshops

Valerie Ellery has served the field of education as a National Board Certified Teacher, curriculum specialist, mentor, reading coach, staff developer, and an award-winning author and consultant. For more information or to reach Valerie, visit www.ValerieEllery.com.

Jennifer L. Rosenboom has been actively involved in teaching and learning as a secondary reading teacher, district administrator in curriculum and professional development, middle school and high school reading coach, and adjunct education instructor at the University of South Florida, Sarasota, Florida. She earned both a bachelor's degree and a master's degree in education from the University of Florida, Gainesville, and a doctorate of education degree in curriculum and instruction from Argosy University in Sarasota.

Jennifer was awarded the 1999 Presidential Regional Award for Reading and Technology, presented annually by IRA, and she is proud to be a national trainer for Project CRISS. She has written multiple literacy instructional guides targeting adolescent readers and is a coauthor of the 2009 Professional Development Facilitator's Guide to Farstrup and Samuels's (2002) *What Research Has to Say About Reading Instruction* (third edition) published by IRA.

Jennifer's passion for effective secondary instruction and learning stem from her 30 years of varied experience in classroom instruction, curriculum development, teacher professional development, writing, and instructional coaching. She currently serves as an educational consultant, supporting inner-city schools and districts as a reading consultant and instructional coach.

Jennifer resides in Parrish, Florida, where she cherishes spending time with family, including her husband, four grown children, daughters-in-law, and two beautiful granddaughters, as well as friends and church family. Jennifer also enjoys horseback riding.

Author Information for Correspondence and Workshops

Jennifer Rosenboom continues to support the field of adolescent literacy through professional development coaching and teacher mentoring. She is dedicated to having an impact on instruction and learning. For more information or to reach Jennifer, visit www .JenniferRosenboom.com.

I always appreciate books written by teachers, particularly when I am in the hands of masters. Valerie Ellery and Jennifer Rosenboom have spent their professional lives helping children become literate adults. They have taught in public schools and have worked as curriculum specialists. Most important, they are teacher mentors. Their rich and varied experiences are captured within the pages of this book. They know students; they know teachers. They take us into classrooms and show us how to nurture and sustain adolescent learners.

Given recent reports about the need to improve adolescent literacy, this resource could not have arrived at a more opportune time. Too many of our young adults are not succeeding academically. Too many students are not completing high school. With the current surge of interest in adolescent literacy, *Sustaining Strategic Readers: Techniques for Supporting Content Literacy in Grades 6–12* meets an important need. Even though the focus is on adolescent literacy, this work transcends grade levels and content areas. Middle grade as well as special needs and content area teachers will find this to be a useful resource.

Upon previewing a draft of this book, I scanned the table of contents and the chapter organization. The content flows from general, more theoretical information about the whole learner to practical strategies focusing on word study, fluency, vocabulary, and comprehension. The first two chapters begin with guiding questions and key terms that provide a purpose for reading. When skimming through Chapters 1 and 2, readers soon discover that essential ideas are captured in headings crafted as questions. Readers know exactly where they are headed. Chapters 3, 4, 5, and 6 begin with a brief overview of research followed by presentations of instructional strategies that include suggestions for teacher talk aligned to questioning taxonomies to help readers think strategically. The presentations of strategies follow a consistent format: purpose, multiple intelligences, materials, and procedure. The authors avoid jargon and make what is potentially complicated accessible to a wide audience of preservice and practicing teachers. These structural features and straightforward style of writing make this book a useful tool for busy educators.

Although this book contains approaches for helping adolescents meet the ever-increasing demands of complex texts, it also addresses the needs of struggling readers. The chapters on word study and fluency are particularly applicable. Secondary literacy specialists and resource teachers specifically will welcome the rich assortment of ideas for teaching word study (e.g., decoding, morphemic analysis, syllabification) and fluency. The authors have even included a section on spelling. Given that most professional resources on adolescent literacy contain little information about teaching these fundamental skills, this book definitely fulfills an important niche. The chapters on vocabulary and comprehension contain ideas found in many articles I have used over the years as inservice handouts. With *Sustaining Strategic Readers*, I will no longer have to sort through my endless files. Valerie and Jennifer have gathered their ideas into one tidy volume.

—Carol M. Santa
Director of Education, Montana Academy
Past President, International Reading Association

Preface

As we create and sustain strategic readers, we present a resource for modeling strategies and techniques that will empower educators and students to bring meaning to learning. We are in the field applying these strategies in multiple secondary content classrooms. With our combined backgrounds in reading strategies and secondary education, master's degrees in reading and in learning disabilities, doctorate in curriculum and instruction, and more than 50 years in education, *Sustaining Strategic Readers: Techniques for Supporting Content Literacy in Grades 6–12* is our response to the collective voices seeking techniques to be embedded within content area instruction at secondary levels.

Creating Strategic Readers (Ellery, 2009) brought attention to the reading strategies at the elementary level. *Sustaining Strategic Readers* evolved from *Creating Strategic Readers* and extends the focus to instruction in secondary classrooms and to improving school-level literacy leadership. IRA (2008) asserts that "the classroom is the place where teacher knowledge, resources, and students come together to make a difference" (p. 4). Teachers need a wealth of applicable research-based reading strategies with clear examples, relevant content area applications, and instructional practices for effective implementation.

As we strive to advance adolescent literacy instruction and sustain strategic adolescent learners, it is imperative that we implement reading strategies and techniques founded on a solid research base as well as on best classroom practices. This essential resource is designed to meet the needs of middle and high school educators, including literacy coaches, content area teachers, preservice educators, reading teachers, and administrators.

Sustaining Strategic Readers provides high-quality techniques framed around the need for reading to be a social learning experience that is rich in reflection and discussion and is relevant, engaging, and meaningful. Preparing students to actively engage in the processes of reading, critical thinking, and problem solving requires a focused and collaborative effort by the secondary school community (Irvin, Meltzer, Dean, & Mickler, 2010). We encourage educators to use this resource to enrich their "instructional tool box" and better equip themselves in the craft of effective reading support.

Acknowledgments

We would like to express our deepest gratitude to those who joined us on this journey. Your inspiration, support, and expertise will never be forgotten.

From Valerie Ellery:

Special thanks to the following people:

- My husband and best friend, Gregg, to whom I am forever grateful for his love and patience

- My children, Nick and Virginia, Derek, Jacey, and Brooke, who allowed mom to "do her thing" one more time—thanks for your patience

- My granddaughter, "Princess" Evie—the legacy continues because of *you*

- My parents, Roger and Laurie, for instilling in me your strong foundation and faith

- My sister, Connie, who is the best travel partner and support on the road

- My colleague and friend, Jennifer, who kept the fire burning for this project and who shared her wealth of knowledge with love and laughter

From Jennifer Rosenboom:

Special thanks to the following people:

- My husband, Rodney, whose encouragement, love, and support means the world

- My children, Chris and Angela, John and Amanda, Wesley and Sarah, and Tracy, who keep me grounded in what is important

- My beautiful granddaughters, Hannah and Madison, and my niece, Jordan, who focus my attention on the importance of supporting schools to be highly effective

- My mother, Judith, and my in-laws, Carol and Dick, who remain steadfast with love and support

- My sister and friend, Joni, who is also a colleague in education— thanks for all your help on this project and through life

- My colleague and coauthor, Val, whose vision, expertise, and friendship are amazing

From Valerie and Jennifer:

We also would like to express a special thank you to the following friends and colleagues:

- Classroom teachers who provided student samples, photographs, and classroom applications—Diana Buell, Susan Darovec, Bill Kebler, Mandy Kersey, Kristi Latture-Simpson, Joni Olson, Deborah Peters, Debbie Robinson, and Marybeth Witham

- Our "own" graphic designers—Jill Cushing and Michael Keller

- Our church families at Bayside Community Church and First Baptist Church of Palmetto

Our guiding question for this book and for today's secondary educators is, "How do we sustain and enhance the secondary readers that were created in elementary classrooms?" As we continue our journey to create and sustain strategic learners, it is essential to analyze the multitude of educational mandates, theories, research-based practices, and well-meaning initiatives aimed at enhancing student learning. As educators, our collective roles and responsibilities map a systematic course to successfully propel learners in the 21st century. Every effort is needed to maintain the instructional cycle as we assess, plan, implement, and reflect to maximize, rather than undermine, the quality of literacy instruction. Our efforts must focus on guiding the 21st-century learner to embrace interpersonal communications, higher order thinking, new literacies (e.g., technology, social media), and to plan and prioritize for results. These foundations focus on the student's ability to apply valuable reading strategies, such as making critical judgments, processing content vocabulary, and integrating prior knowledge with new knowledge.

Reading Next—A Vision for Action and Research in Middle and High School Literacy (Biancarosa & Snow, 2006) reinforces the need for relevant and effective instruction for secondary learners: "Literacy demands have increased and changed as the technological capabilities of our society have expanded and been made widely available; concomitantly, the need for flexible, self-regulated individuals who can respond to rapidly changing contexts has also increased" (p. 9). These guidelines focus on instructing the whole learner through explicit comprehension instruction, motivation and self-directed learning, and effective instructional principles embedded in ongoing formative and summative assessments. We explore these essential reading components through the lens of a content area educator.

Overview of *Sustaining Strategic Readers*

In *Sustaining Strategic Readers* the reading areas of word study, fluency, vocabulary, and comprehension are outlined. Each area contains relevant techniques to support the strategies, academic vocabulary, and teacher talk presented within a comprehensive secondary literacy framework.

Chapter 1, "Focusing on the Secondary 'Whole' Learner," focuses on the 21st-century whole learner, with emphasis on motivation, student engagement, and building self-regulated adolescent learners.

Chapter 2, "Creating a Comprehensive Structure for Learning," presents a curriculum, assessment, and instruction (CAI) framework and discusses relevant research in adolescent literacy, the conditions for optimal learning in a comprehensive secondary literacy classroom, and assessment.

Chapters 3 through 6 build on specific components of reading aligned for the evident needs of secondary learners (Chapter 3, "Word Study: The Wonder of Words"; Chapter 4, "Fluency: Finding the Flow"; Chapter 5, "Vocabulary: Making Meaningful Connections"; Chapter 6, "Comprehension: Frontloading and Downloading"). Word study is the analysis of word patterns and structures and facilitates reading fluency, vocabulary, and comprehension for accuracy. Fluency is the ability to read with proper phrasing and flow to sound conversational and is the bridge to comprehension. Vocabulary involves students making connections to new and already known information about a word and demonstrating meanings of new words effectively in oral and written communication. Comprehension is the ability to construct meaning in all aspects of reading. It is essential for secondary teachers and students develop an understanding of these literacy components, as they characterize the processes of effective readers and build the foundation for content understanding and discovery.

Each chapter focuses on a component, offers an overview of the component, and identifies strategies with accompanying techniques for implementation and application. The Appendix provides resources and reproducibles to support educators in implementing the techniques, and the References and Index support educators in accessing and using the text.

Embedded strategy assessments support educators in checking for understanding and collecting evidence of student learning. The CAI framework is demonstrated in each chapter, and teacher understanding is supported through relevant secondary vignettes (teaching examples) in varied areas of content instruction. Relevant research is presented in the initial sections of each chapter, validating the content and aligning with Response to Intervention (RTI) and current reading initiatives. A review of appropriate statements, questions, and prompts (teacher talk) is included for each strategy and accompanying techniques. Using teacher talk aligned both to Bloom's taxonomy (Anderson & Krathwohl, 2001; Bloom, 1956) of questions, statements, and prompts and to Webb's (1999) depth-of-knowledge (DOK) levels encourages readers to think strategically and supports teachers in generating effective inquiry and reflection.

The techniques within each strategy section list the technique's purpose, materials needed, relevant multiple intelligences (Gardner, 1993), and procedure. Most techniques have a supplemental procedure for motivation and engagement. The Motivation/Engagement section identifies and uses one of the multiple intelligences other than those that are highlighted in the main procedure of the technique.

Accompanying resources, reproducibles, and matrixes enable teachers to efficiently and effectively enhance understanding for challenged learners as well as maximize learning for all students. This organizational structure is ideally aligned to the subject matter by providing a secure foundation of relevant adolescent reading research, addressing all content areas of instruction, providing adaptable graphics, and, most important, presenting theory and practice clearly in one text.

Chapter 1

Focusing on the Secondary "Whole" Learner

Guiding Questions

- What are the characteristics and instructional needs of the 21st-century secondary learner?
- What are essential considerations in meeting the literacy needs of adolescent learners?
- How can we effectively motivate and engage secondary readers?

Key Terms

- **Metacognitive Thinking:** Consciousness of one's thought and learning processes ("thinking about thinking"). This reinforces understanding the purpose of a lesson and the usefulness of a technique.
- **21st-Century Literacy**: Reading, writing, listening, viewing, and speaking of and with traditional texts and media and also with new social, digital, visual, and informational texts and media.
- **21st-Century Secondary Learner:** One who exhibits a wide mental grasp of the whole-learner standards (e.g., effective communicator, critical thinker) and uses a variety of multiple intelligences.
- **Whole Learner:** A 21st-century secondary learner whose developmental domains are interdependent and occur simultaneously. These developmental domains are the learner's creative/cognitive growth, intellectual/mental and physical health, and social and emotional welfare.

It is our belief that by weaving the challenges surfacing from past educational mandates with instructional guidelines and research-based practices we can effectively educate the secondary whole learner. The focus of *Sustaining Strategic Readers* is to embrace the challenge of educating 21st-century adolescent learners by building and sustaining secondary literacy competency in the areas of word study, fluency, vocabulary, and comprehension. It is time for targeted literacy embedded in content area instruction. As secondary educators, we are called to meet the learning needs of a diverse community of learners by cultivating our students to become strategic, motivated, engaged, technologically literate, and self-directed learners.

What Are the Characteristics and Instructional Needs of the 21st-Century Secondary Learner?

The ultimate goal is for learners to exhibit a wide mental grasp of the 21st-century literacies. We need to reach and teach the whole learner. By *whole learner*, we are referring to a 21st-century secondary learner whose developmental domains are interdependent and occur simultaneously. Figure 1.1 illustrates the composition of a 21st-century secondary learner. To

FIGURE 1.1. Composition of a 21st-Century Secondary Learner

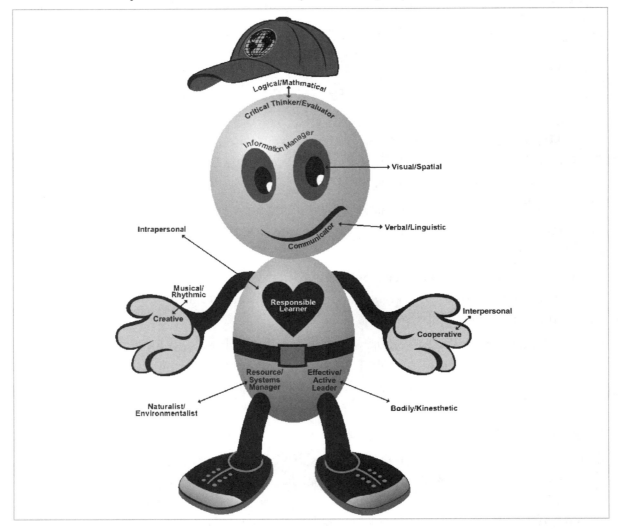

teach the whole learner, educators have to know *who* they are teaching. Table 1.1 describes a way of looking at the components of a whole learner. Educators can use this framework to SPICE up their understanding of the developmental domains of the whole learner. Responsive educators recognize that adolescents "deserve educational experiences and schools that are organized to address their unique physical, intellectual, emotional/ psychological, moral/ethical, and social developmental characteristics and needs" (Caskey & Anfara, 2007, p. 3).

The whole-learner standards are the processes and abilities that help the 21st-century secondary learner apply specific content knowledge to real-world situations. These standards are information manager, communicator, critical thinker/evaluator, creative learner, effective/ active leader, cooperative worker, responsible learner, and resource/systems manager. Table 1.2 describes the multiple intelligences aligned to these whole-learner standards. According to Gardner (1999), "Intelligence is a biopsychological potential to process information that can be activated in a cultural setting to solve problems or create products that are of value in a culture" (p. 34). The multiple intelligences are comprehensive categories of different ways to demonstrate intellectual ability.

When educators assess the whole learner using the lenses of multiple intelligences, whole-learner standards, and the SPICE developmental domains, the evidence they glean will guide the educators toward reaching and teaching their students successfully. We know that all students do not think and learn the same way.

TABLE 1.1. Adding SPICE to the Developmental Domains of the Whole Learner

Domain	Description
S Social health (personality/social skills)	The ability to form attachments, associate with others, cooperate, share, and create lasting relationships in a structured environment for socialization.
P Physical health (body)	The development of fine (small) and gross (large) motor skills. Psychological changes that occur in the body, such as puberty.
I Intellectual/mental health	The ability to sense the world through an intellectual (thought and reason) capacity. Innate sense of curiosity and wonder.
C Creative/cognitive growth	The development of special abilities and creative talents, such as music, art, writing, and reading. It is a way for self-expression and a springboard for problem solving.
E Emotional welfare (feelings and behaviors)	Development of self-awareness, self-confidence, and the ability to cope with one's feelings, as well as having empathy for others.

Note. Adapted from Godbey, 2008

TABLE 1.2. Comprehensive Multiple Intelligences Matrix

Whole-Child Standards/Multiple Intelligences	ABILITIES What they are able to do…	INTERESTS What they like to do…	MOTIVATION How to enthuse them…	COGNITIVE ENGAGEMENT How they actively think…	TEACHER TALK How to communicate with them…	ASSESSMENT How to know if they can do it…
VISUAL Spatial (Information Manager)	• Perceive the visual; locate and organize relevant information; relate to size, area, or positions	• Design • Draw, doodle • Observe • Paint	• Cartoons • Collages • Images • Multimedia • Visual aids • Virtual reality games	In pictures… • Mental images • Graphic organizers • Spatial orientation	• Visualizing in mind's eye • Illustrating • Interpreting • Representing	• Visual metaphors and analogies • Checklists • Graphs • Rubrics
VERBAL Linguistic (Communicator)	• Communicate for a given purpose, subject matter, and audience; storyteller	• Read and write • Format stories • Write in a diary • Debate • Tell stories	• Best-selling books • Word games • Blogs/wikis • Peer counseling • Humor • Dialogue	With words… • Elaborative • Expressive • Symbolism	• Convincing • Describing • Explaining • Translating • Identifying • Listing	• Surveys • Interviews • Word associations • Linguistic humor
LOGICAL Mathematical (Critical Thinker/Evaluator)	• Use reason and identify problems that need new and different solutions	• Experiments • Puzzles • Brain teasers • Analyze abstract relationships	• Graphing • Evaluating • Calculating • Exploring • Researching	• Reasoning, inductive and deductive • Quantifying • Critically • Logically	• Analyzing • Calculating • Distinguishing • Verifying • Comparing and contrasting	• Strategic games • Matrices • Mnemonics • Spreadsheets • Problem solve
MUSICAL Rhythmic (Creative Learner)	• Create, understand, and communicate intuitively through music	• Sing and hum • Listen to music • Jingles and raps • Improvise • Compose	• Audiorecording • Rhythms • Musical instruments • Choral reading	• By melody or rhythm patterns	• Creating • Demonstrating • Expressing • Performing	• Tonal patterns • Musical performances • Checklists • Compositions
BODILY Kinesthetic (Effective/Active Leader)	• Control body movements, handle objects, multitask	• Sports • Dancing • Working with hands • Creating things	• Acting • Field trips • Active learning • Role-play	• Interactively • Physically • Globally • Collaboratively	• Acting out • Constructing • Creating • Dramatizing	• Projects • Interviews • Dramatizations
INTER/PERSONAL (Cooperative Worker)	• Recognize and respond to others' moods, motivations, and desires	• Spend time helping others • E-mail, text • Community events	• Reporting • Dialogue • Debate • Peer teaching	• Communicating • Self-reflecting • Metacognitively • Through simulations	• Brainstorming • Role-playing • Sharing • Collaborating	• Group projects • Discussions • Paraphrasing • Buzz sessions
INTRA/PERSONAL (Responsible Learner)	• Self-reflect and have awareness of one's own strengths and weaknesses	• Plan • Imagine • Think time • Problem solve	• Journaling • Learning logs • Independent learning • Goal setting	• In relation to self • Reflection • Imagery	• Concentrating • Imagining • Self-reflecting • Rehearsing "I" statements	• Self-assessments • Independent contracts • Portfolios
NATURALIST Environmentalist (Resource/Systems Manager)	• Distinguish among features of environment	• Backpack • Nature walks • Visit zoos	• Interacting with plants, animals, and other objects in nature	• Systematic • Orderly • Environmental	• Classifying • Analyzing • Investigating	• Charts • Graphs • Systems • Scavenger hunt lists • Classification graphic organizers

It is important to recognize that different learners learn best at different times with different contents and in different contexts. Therefore, a one-size-fits-all, "high-stakes" achievement test may still leave educators and students motivated by the score and not the process of learning (Ellery, 2009, p. 16).

It is imperative that we assess the learner's style and align the proper instructional design to bridge success. There have been numerous studies and findings that refer to the various learning styles that influence students' abilities to make sense of the experience, gain deep understanding, and achieve academic goals (Caine & Caine, 2007; Coffield, Moseley, Hall, & Ecclestone, 2004; Hodgkinson, 2006; Jensen & Nickelsen, 2008; Kohn, 2005; Levine, 2002; Maslow, 1943; O'Connor & Jackson, 2008; Zigler & Finn-Stevenson, 2007).

As we use assessments to gauge what our learners know and need to know, it is necessary that the first step is to *know* our learners. The whole-learner standards and multiple intelligences support educators in discovering the best practices and assessments for achieving this goal. The techniques presented in this book are based on the foundational design of instructing with the knowledge of the whole-learner standards and intelligences to create a comprehensive learning environment.

What Are Essential Considerations in Meeting the Literacy Needs of Adolescent Learners?

The past decade has evinced growing interest in and research on how to most effectively instruct adolescent learners. Adolescents are characterized by their unique literacy needs, which include the following:

- Experiences with relevant and diverse texts
- Opportunities for building relationships
- Discussion and critical thinking opportunities
- Motivating and engaging learning experiences
- A sense of autonomy and identity

(Bean & Harper, 2009; Lenski & Lewis, 2008; National Council of Teachers of English [NCTE], 2004)

As students make the transition into middle school, they encounter academic content discourse in science, mathematics, and social studies, and therefore require richer and more engaging reading instruction (Bean & Harper, 2009; NCTE, 2004). The changing literacy needs of adolescents require instruction in understanding and using complex content materials as well as instructional support for many secondary learners in basic literacy. It is beneficial for secondary teachers to understand the unique needs of adolescent learners and their intellectual development as they align instructional practices to address these characteristics. In The National Middle School Association's research summary, Caskey and Anfara (2007) describe intellectual development in terms of learners' abilities to understand, reason, and apply abstract thought processes.

How Can We Effectively Motivate and Engage Secondary Readers?

Educators strive to instruct in a manner that intrinsically motivates and engages students through the learning process. Secondary educators we have encountered confirm a decline in the number of readers who are motivated to read compared with the number of motivated readers in elementary classrooms. According to Irvin, Meltzer, Mickler, Phillips, and Dean (2009),

> Too often, content area reading and writing assignments engage students in only a cursory way with content. Reading a chapter and answering the questions, writing a formulaic lab report, writing an essay about a topic that is not of interest to the writer, or reading an article and writing a summary are typical content reading and writing assignments that tend to hinder students' active engagement with the content. In addition, assignments that are too vague or too open may not support students' investment in thinking deeply about the content. (p. 16)

To instruct to the whole learner, educators must be keenly aware of the abilities, interests, motivation, and multiple intelligences of the learner. The *ability* of a learner refers to what the student is able to do. *Interest* is what the student wants to do. *Motivation* is what gives the student a reason or passion for a certain behavior. *Engagement* is how the student actively thinks.

To illustrate how a learner can move through the process of having the ability to do something and then becoming engaged in doing it, let us use an analogy of house cleaning. You may have the *ability* to clean your house, but you choose to lie on the couch and watch television. The *interest* may even be there to clean the house. You *want* a clean house, but you are not *motivated* to do the work, so you stay on the couch. But imagine that the telephone rings and your friends say they are on their way over to your house. You now have a *motivation* to get of the couch and start to tidy up. However, you are not thinking about where you are shoving items; you are trying to get the surfaces cleared. To be fully *engaged* in cleaning, you would need to be actively thinking about how best to organize and clean to increase peace in your life.

When educators consider the engagement of the learner, student achievement increases (Brophy, 1983; Dewey, 1913; Fink & Samuels, 2008; Harackiewicz, Durik, Barron, Linnenbrink-Garcia, & Tauer, 2008; Jang, 2008; Jensen, 2005; Kohn, 1993; Lavoie, 2007; Skinner & Belmont, 1993). Table 1.3 highlights the concepts of interest, motivation, and engagement. Educators can use the questions within each of these categories as they design lessons that support learners to engage in the learning process. The goal for adolescent

TABLE 1.3. Interest, Motivation, and Engagement

Interest	Motivation	Engagement
The degree to which the student demonstrates curiosity, drive, and passion about the task.	The factors that stimulate and give incentive (intrinsic and extrinsic), reason, and desire for a certain behavior.	The degree to which the student is actively connected to and thinking about the learning experience.
<ul><li>What are the student's passions?</li><li>What is the student doing after school or in his or her free time?</li><li>What does the student talk about or express most?</li><li>When does the student become involved with coming up with answers and responses?</li></ul>	<ul><li>Why did the student behave or act the way he or she did?</li><li>Does the student initiate action when given the opportunity?</li><li>Is the student exerting intense effort in the learning tasks?</li><li>Is the student demonstrating enthusiasm and curiosity toward the given learning experience?</li></ul>	<ul><li>Is the student willingly participating?</li><li>Does the student genuinely care about the learning experience?</li><li>Is the student actively involved in the outcome of the experience?</li><li>Does the student share in the responses of his or her learning?</li></ul>

Note. Adapted from Ellery, V. (2009). *Creating strategic readers: Techniques for developing competency in phonemic awareness, phonics, fluency, vocabulary, and comprehension* (2nd ed.). Newark, DE: International Reading Association.

learners is to become autonomous learners. Autonomous learners can be self-regulated learners, which is the ultimate goal of a strategic reader (Hilden & Pressley, 2007; Paris, Wasik, & Turner, 1991; Parsons, 2008).

To instruct the whole learner, educators need to know the necessary strategies, which we refer to as the *curriculum component* for secondary readers; know their learners, which we refer to as *assessment with teacher talk*; and know which techniques, which we refer to as *instruction*, will support the needs of their learners. The techniques can represent the specific skills and instruction designed to support a strategy.

Chapter 2

Creating a Comprehensive Structure for Learning

Guiding Questions

- How does the alignment of curriculum, instruction, and assessment support effective literacy instruction?
- What knowledge and strategies do learners need to be successful readers?
- How can assessment inform meaningful literacy instruction?
- What is the purpose and scope of intervention processes in middle and high schools?
- How can high-quality literacy techniques support the essential strategies of secondary learners?

Key Terms

- **Assessment:** Gathering evidence to determine what the student knows and still needs to know (behavior indicators and teacher talk in Chapters 3–6).
- **Content Area Literacy:** The ability to use reading and writing for the acquisition of new content in a given discipline (e.g., mathematics, science) and to interpret, evaluate, and communicate information in the discipline.
- **Curriculum:** What the student is expected to know and be able to do (strategies in Chapters 3–6).
- **Instruction:** Methods for reaching the readers to ensure that learning occurs (techniques in Chapters 3–6).
- **Strategy:** An ongoing cognitive process encompassing specific skills for content learning; a method toward the goal.
- **Teacher Talk:** Statements, questions, and prompts applied in conversational coaching to encourage reflection and higher levels of thinking.
- **Technique:** An instructional procedure applied to differentiate learning to support strategic reading.

Comprehensive secondary literacy builds on a solid CAI foundation focused on aligning literacy and content learning. According to Parris, Fisher, and Headley (2009), "Content literacy requires skills to extract information and understand concepts in a particular discipline" (p. 9). Curriculum, assessment, and instruction are interwoven, guiding students to become independent learners in academic areas, and they are crucial for enhancing student achievement. Our goal is to educate the whole student through modeling, scaffolding, and applying technological resources. As educators of adolescents, we must commit to exhibiting a grasp of the literacy skills and processes required for secondary students in multiple disciplines. Mraz, Rickelman, and Vacca (2009) state, "Content area reading is no longer regarded by most experts as a matter of reading information from a single textbook. Instead, students must seek, evaluate, and comprehend information from a variety of print and technology sources" (p. 85).

Assessment results validate that some middle and high school students struggle with academic reading. Secondary teachers can provide challenging content literacy instruction that meets the specific demands of their content area while supporting a common instructional language to help students make connections across subjects (Irvin et al., 2009; Moore, 2009). Every subject requires some form of reading, and content teachers should use techniques most appropriate for their area of instruction (Fawcett & Rasinski, 2008). Content area teachers can enhance literacy by taking a leadership role in defining how reading is taught without taking time away from their content curriculum. Irvin and colleagues reinforce that content teachers can make a distinct difference for their students by "shifting instruction from a sole focus on learning content knowledge to the goal of learning content through strengthening content literacy" (p. 41).

C = Curriculum

The initial aspect of CAI within the comprehensive content literacy classroom is curriculum. Educators use a standards-based curriculum as a guide in determining what they want students to know and be able to do. The mission statement for the Common Core State Standards is to

> provide a consistent, clear understanding of what students are expected to learn, so teachers and parents know what they need to do to help them. The standards are designed to be robust and relevant to the real world, reflecting the knowledge and skills that our young people need for success in college and careers. With American students fully prepared for the future, our communities will be best positioned to compete successfully in the global economy. (National Governors Association Center for Best Practices and Council of Chief State School Officers, 2010, p. 1)

These national standards for major subject areas are initiated to work toward states and schools having clear, consistent, and challenging standards of achievement and accountability. These evidenced-based core standards are drafted to define the knowledge and skills students need to be successful in college academic courses, the workforce, and in a global economy (Common Core State Standards Initiative, 2010).

Clearly communicated standards-based learning targets presented in student-friendly language provide educators and students with a purpose for learning. By crafting instruction using current standards, teachers set and express measurable learning goals that can be used to monitor student progress and applaud successes. Marzano (2010) clarifies the significance of goal setting by stating, "Certainly one generalization is that setting clear and specific goals for learning that are at just the right level of difficulty can greatly enhance student achievement" (p. 12). *Sustaining Strategic Readers* focuses the secondary educator to apply strategies, techniques, and teacher talk within the reading components of word study, fluency, vocabulary, and comprehension. These components are infused within current national (Common Core) and state standards and aligned benchmarks.

What Knowledge and Strategies Do Learners Need to Be Successful Readers?

Table 2.1 identifies the strategies within secondary components that are highlighted in Chapters 3–6. These strategies are enduring common threads that withstand ongoing reading initiatives and programs to support proficient readers. Strategic readers embrace the text and bring meaning to what they are reading. These readers apply reading skills automatically, concentrating on the strategies rather than skills.

A baseball analogy clarifies the relationship between strategies and skills. The first step in becoming a great baseball player is for the person to want to be a proficient baseball player and understand the "why" behind the practices. Coaches instill right away what it takes to be a baseball player—hitting the ball, fielding, and running the bases. These are the strategies, the methods toward the goal. Each strategy encompasses specific skills necessary

TABLE 2.1. Reading Components and Aligned Strategies

Word Study	Fluency	Vocabulary	Comprehension
• Synthesizing • Analyzing affixes • Analyzing root words • Spelling	• Phrasing • Scaffolding and Rereading • Expressing • Pacing • Wide reading	• Associating • Contextualizing • Visualizing • Personalizing • Referencing	• Previewing • Activating and Connecting • Predicting • Inquiring and Inferring • Determining importance • Summarizing and Synthesizing

to achieve success with it. Baseball players practice individual skills (e.g., positioning of feet, follow-through with swing, changing up position for specific pitches) to become proficient with the strategies. Skills are for drill, not "drill and kill." When learners know why they are practicing the skill, the skill does not kill their motivation to continue engagement with the routine.

Therefore, during practice, learners are more apt to remain engaged when they know that each practice is increasing their chances to become successful in reaching the goal. To be successful on game day, players need to "step up to the plate" and become batters, focusing on the end result—hitting the ball successfully. In doing so, the players use the hitting strategy while applying all of the batting skills acquired in practice and continuing to problem solve while at bat (e.g., changing swing for a curve ball). Authentic practice on the field means having all of the tools necessary (e.g., bat, ball, field) rather than just hearing about playing ball.

Similarly, students practice reading skills necessary for all content area reading (e.g., affixes, reading rate, skim and scan) that support reading strategies (e.g., analyzing words, pacing, previewing). The students also focus on the end goal, which is reading for meaning. In doing so, the students are using the reading strategies while applying all of the skills acquired in authentic practice and continuing to problem solve while reading. This is strategic reading. Metacognitive learners know the stages in the process of learning and understand their preferred approaches to it. They can articulate what they need to do to attain learning goals, and they apply strategies to become successful learners: "Students who achieve well in school know when they have understood, and they know how to employ a variety of strategies to attain meaning" (Santa, 2006, p. 469). Knowing which strategy to apply to comprehend content text allows students to demonstrate their grasp of the curriculum.

Strategy instruction should be embedded within targeted content planning and instruction to support students in making connections among ideas in text (McKeown, Beck, & Blake, 2009). Content literacy and learning are interconnected in the secondary curriculum in various content areas: "Supporting readers as they grapple with the highly specific demands of texts written for different content-areas will help prepare them for citizenship, encourage personal growth and life-satisfaction on many levels, and open up opportunities for further education and employment" (Lee & Spratley, 2010, p. 2). The purpose of literacy is the learning of essential content, and literacy is at the core of secondary curriculum. The commonalities of thinking, reading, and writing underpin the content areas. According to Shanahan and Shanahan (2008), "The different disciplines result in unique challenges for readers" (p. 53). Multimodal learning is necessary for students to meet the challenges of varied forms of text across disciplines. These varied text representations, including digital media and artistic designs, are integral components of 21st-century society as well as a part of the meaning-making process of secondary learners (Ellery, 2009; Jewitt & Kress, 2003; Thompson, 2008; Unsworth & Heberle, 2009). The shift from elementary to secondary school brings with it modifications in the "nature of literacy requirements" (NCTE, 2006,

p. 3). Appropriate interventions and literacy support in content classrooms benefit secondary learners, and our goal should be to provide relevant opportunities for adolescent learners to become engaged in their learning, apply the curriculum, and strategically discover meaning in all content classrooms (Scammacca et al., 2007).

A = Assessment

Assessment is the next component in CAI comprehensive content literacy classrooms. In *Understanding and Using Reading Assessment, K–12*, Afflerbach (2007) reminds us "that reading assessment must have the primary consequence of helping students continue their development as readers" (p. 18). Students and teachers should use a variety of assessments appropriate to their learning environments and should accommodate the assessment purposes (Edwards, Turner, & Mokhtari, 2008; Ellery, 2009; NCTE, 2004). Assessments are essential to determine students' current knowledge base (i.e., strengths and weaknesses), to inform instruction, and to motivate and engage students.

How Can Assessment Inform Meaningful Literacy Instruction?

Educators need to reflect on the purpose of assessment. There is an old proverb that states, "You don't fatten a sheep by weighing it." A shepherd has to tend to and feed his sheep for the flock to grow strong and produce sufficient wool; otherwise, the sheep would not develop properly from lack of nutrition and care. This proverb applies to our students today in the assessment arena of the 21st-century classroom. Educators need time to feed their "sheep" (a.k.a. students) through proper instruction so they can grow academically. A disservice is done when educators assess only to receive raw-score data that is not evaluated to inform instruction. When educators record their student data into their record books or online and continue covering the curriculum without evaluating the data, giving feedback to the students, and using the data to inform instruction, their students have a greater chance of falling into a cycle of failure (Ellery, 2009; Stanovich, 1986). The assessment loses the ability to become a tool for learning and for focusing on the depth of understanding of the learners.

Stanovich (1986) resurfaces the concept of the Matthew effect, which has been frequently related to the failure cycle in reading. The *Matthew effect*, a term which was first coined by Merton (1968), is related to the biblical passage conveying that the rich get richer and the poor get poorer. When applied to reading, this concept translates as "those who read, read more, and those who do not read, do not read." According to Stanovich, the students who are reading well and who have good vocabularies will read more, learn word meanings, and hence read even better. Children with inadequate vocabularies—who read slowly and without enjoyment—will read less, and as a result have slower development of vocabulary knowledge, which inhibits further growth in reading. (p. 381)

In other words, as readers encounter difficulties that hinder their reading, the experience becomes less rewarding and can lead to a lack of desire to read. With fewer reading experiences, these learners fall further behind in their development as readers, therefore setting into motion the failure cycle. In his *Reading Research Quarterly* article, Stanovich (1986) questions for further research to determine if "instructional differences are a factor in generating Matthew Effects" (p. 396). Research shows astounding evidence that instructional differences do make a major impact on the reciprocal relationships (Marzano, Pickering, & Pollock, 2001; Nye, Konstantopoulos, & Hedges, 2004).

Assessment is an integral part of effective instruction and a common process for providing students with feedback (Marzano, 2010). Educators and students use multiple types of assessments to reflect on how learning is progressing, see where improvements can be made, and identify next steps. Screening assessments are provided for the general student population so educators can determine deficit areas in students' performances. The National Center on Response to Intervention (2010) defines *screening* as

brief assessments that are valid, reliable, and evidence-based. They are conducted with all students or targeted groups of students to identify those who are at risk of academic failure and likely needing additional or alternative forms of instruction to supplement the conventional general education approach. (p. 8)

Effective teaching requires using varied forms of assessments to guide decision making and dig deeper to understand student needs. Analyzing multiple assessments is analogous to the frog overlays found in decades of biology textbooks. You begin with a photograph of a frog, and as you add overlays, you see the muscular system, followed by the internal organs, and then the circulatory system. Each layer enriches the view and deepens understanding. Analyses of varied forms of student assessment data provide more windows to guide our instructional practices. This assessment process "keeps students and their teachers in touch with understanding and achievement on a continuous basis, allowing them to know what specific actions they can take to improve learning every day" (Stiggins & Chappuis, 2008, p. 44). Systematically collected and analyzed student data can be used to determine if students are making adequate progress toward learning goals and gauge the effectiveness of instruction. The National Research Center on Learning Disabilities clarifies that progress monitoring should assess the specific skills contained in state standards, be administered repeatedly over shorter periods of time, be applicable to monitor student progress over time, and remain relevant for development of instructional strategies and techniques to address the specific areas of need (Johnson, Mellard, Fuchs, & McNight, 2006).

Assessing Through Conversational Coaching

Conversational coaching is referred to as "teacher talk" throughout this book, and it is embedded in all of the strategies. These statements, questions, and prompts are tools for conversations as educators coach their students in thinking and reading strategically. Students who are given the opportunity to process information through higher order thinking comprehend and store the knowledge for future authentic application far more than students who are responding passively to lower order questions (Amer, 2006; Anderson & Krathwohl, 2001; Bloom, 1956; Eber, 2007; Ellery, 2009; Kunen, Cohen, & Solman, 1981; Redfield & Rousseau, 1981; Taylor, 2008). Asking students to reflect on and respond to the global understanding of why they are learning specific content is necessary in bringing them to a metacognitive awareness (the ability to think about their learning process).

Chapters 3–6 demonstrate a leveling of teacher talk with each of the component strategies to support deeper learning. The teacher talk is aligned to Bloom's taxonomy (i.e., creating, evaluating, analyzing, applying, understanding, remembering; Anderson & Krathwohl, 2001) and the hierarchy of Webb's (1999) DOK levels (i.e., recall, skills/concepts, strategic, extended). Merging the DOK levels extends the taxonomy to determine the context in which the verbs are used and the depth of thinking is required. These levels of thinking describe the progression of what is being taught and learned. According to Confucius, a Chinese philosopher, "He who learns but does not think, is lost! He who thinks but does not learn is in great danger."

I = Instruction

The final component of the CAI comprehensive classroom is instruction. Effective instruction is all about the "how"—how to ensure that a wide mental grasp of the "what," which is the curriculum, is occurring with the learner. This is accomplished through concise, meaningful, and, at times, differentiated ways educators engage all learners. Instruction refers to approaches of teaching as well as the learning techniques used to support students' abilities to self-regulate the content and outcomes specified by a curriculum. This goes far beyond covering the content, as educators guide students to comprehend the curriculum. Effective instruction is responsive to the learners' needs. It has a system in place for gradual release of responsibility (Pearson & Gallagher, 1983), in which the learning evolves from teacher-directed support to student-directed learning. Table 2.2 describes the strategic learning plan's instructional components of preparation, initiation, consideration, collaboration, application, reflection, and intersession. This format provides secondary content teachers with an instructional planning guide to ensure that lessons focus on establishing a conducive learning environment (Cambourne, 1995), targeted learning objectives, active learning, collaboration, and reflection on learning.

TABLE 2.2. Instructional Components of the Strategic Learning Plan

Component	Description
Preparation	• Determine the topic, concept, content, or goal and align to standards. • Write clear purpose or objective and determine the "why." • Prepare instructional materials and establish an environment conducive for learning.
Initiation	• Create an action that sets the stage for learning. • Establish an anticipatory lead-in or grabber. • Develop student interest.
Consideration	• Demonstrate in a clear way meaningful initial instruction. • Explain and model the "what," "how," and "why" of the task. • Provide detailed examination of content.
Collaboration	• Provide instructional format for interaction among learners. • Support flexible grouping for student teamwork. • Engage learners in a shared and guided experience.
Application	• Establish opportunities for partner and independent practice. • Make available clear step-by-step procedures for self-regulation. • Provide experiences for active engagement and approximations.
Reflection	• Provide a time for students to consider what they have learned and what they would like to learn. • Think about the anticipatory set from the initiation and reflect on the learning process.
Intersession	• Present other outside assignments or independent work for continued practice.

Chapters 3–6 incorporate a variety of techniques to support the reading strategies and align with the needs of the learners. The strategies and techniques are listed at the beginning of each chapter. Each technique starts with stating the purpose (the "why") and is followed by the corresponding multiple intelligences that are incorporated to instruct the whole learner. It is critical that the teacher respond with immediate intense instructional intervention if a student demonstrates levels of weakness in an area. This response accelerates the "mending and repairing" process to bring wholeness to the student experiencing fragmented learning.

What Is the Purpose and Scope of Intervention Processes in Middle and High Schools?

The necessity for effective intervention is driven home in the story of Sam (pseudonym), Jennifer's former student. Sam was identified as having a specific learning disability (SLD) when he was in the primary grades; he evinced a significant discrepancy between IQ and achievement, and processing deficits were identified. His elementary grades were characterized by regular classroom placement, daily pull-out for SLD small-group instruction, individualized educational plans, and retentions in both second and fifth grades. For Sam, middle school meant targeted learning strategy classes, mainstream coursework, summer school, and ongoing struggles in decoding and comprehending content texts, often at his frustration level. By high school, Sam was two years older than his grade-level peers.

During Sam's freshman year, a social studies teacher, working with the reading coach, began to model and infuse techniques and strategies to support students to effectively use social studies content text. Sam began to understand the need to self-monitor, establish background knowledge, preview text structure, explore word structures, and track his progress as a fluent reader. Jennifer clearly remembers this young man exclaiming, "I can do this! Why didn't you show me how to do this before now?" As secondary educators, we may be the "last, best chance" for success. How many students such as Sam are in need of intervention in high school content classrooms?

Effective educators are cognizant of learners' needs and reach into their "toolboxes" for multifaceted techniques that support responsive literacy instruction. Intervention processes are being explored by some middle and high schools to improve student achievement outcomes through common elements. Canter, Klotz, and Cowan (2008) capture the following common elements of intervention programs:

- Systematic data collection

- Staff support and training

- Applications of high-quality instructional strategies and techniques

- Collaborative teams

- Parental involvement and coordination and integrations with existing scheduling and intervention programs

A growing body of research on secondary applications of RTI is guiding secondary educators to provide a mechanism for supporting struggling students. Initially designed to provide a systematic and comprehensive evaluation for learning disabilities (LD), RTI is a research-based instructional process that analyzes learning over time and informs decisions about appropriate interventions and the nature of instruction (Allington & Walmsley, 2007; Duffy, 2007). Secondary-level RTI findings are preliminary and focus on reading and writing, yet these approaches may expand beyond a literacy focus and guide secondary school implementation of RTI.

While varied models of RTI exist, a common conceptual framework focuses on the use of high-quality instructional practices, screening and progress-monitoring measures, and data analysis. An emerging body of research recognizes that intervention may include a multitiered intervention approach based on the progress monitoring of struggling adolescent learners. As students get older, they can fall further and further behind. What is essential is the idea that we address the needs of most learners by providing high-quality and culturally responsive instruction in the least intrusive environment (Canter et al., 2008; Duffy, 2009;

Ehren & Laster, 2010; Fuchs & Fuchs, 2008; Johnston, 2010, National High School Center, National Center on Response to Intervention and Center of Instruction, 2010; Rebora, 2010).

Secondary school implementation presents several challenges because of the structure, organization, and culture of middle and high schools. However, according to IRA's Response to Intervention Commission (2010), RTI "must be a part of a comprehensive, systemic approach to language and literacy assessment and instruction that supports all preK–12 students and teachers" (p. 4). Although the essential components of RTI may be consistent, the strategies for implementation may differ. Common implementation hurdles noted by schools include scheduling, staff "buy-in," teacher professional development, availability of resources, and analysis of the fidelity of implementation. Despite these challenges, secondary schools are exploring interventions to address instruction, assessment, use of multiple intervention tiers, and determining research-based services, techniques, and strategies to provide at each level (National High School Center, National Center on Response to Intervention and Center of Instruction, 2010; Rozalski, 2010).

Figure 2.1 is a model of intervention and captures key components as well as initial planning and implementations by secondary schools who have ventured ahead with RTI.

FIGURE 2.1. Model of Intervention

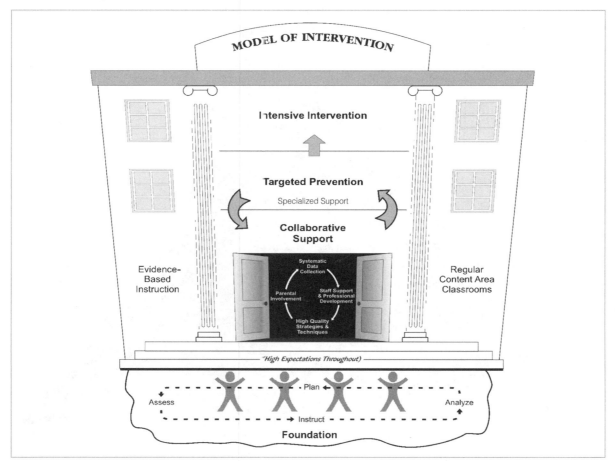

The multitiered approaches are possible models for adaptation and integration. The techniques presented in this book are designed to support research-based strategies to sustain strategic readers at each level as we provide responsive literacy intervention for secondary learners.

The Challenge

Curriculum, assessment, and instruction are core infrastructure components that align to create a highly effective, engaging, and powerful comprehensive content literacy classroom. Figure 2.2 illustrates the cohesive CAI alignment, with the 21st-century secondary learner at the core of the planning and decision-making process. The responsibility for instructing basic reading skills is a task for the reading teacher and specialist, but content teachers can support students toward becoming responsible and strategic readers, critical thinkers, and effective communicators (Irvin et al., 2009).

FIGURE 2.2. Curriculum, Assessment, and Instruction (CAI) Model

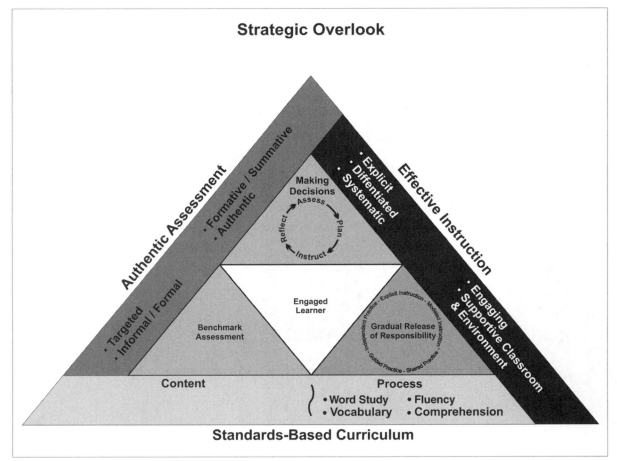

Educators must meet the challenge to identify the strengths and weaknesses of their students and know how to motivate and engage them in the learning process. Using varied formative assessments to guide instruction allows us to enhance our instructional toolboxes and repertoires of strategies, techniques, and teacher talk to meet the unique needs of our secondary learners. Our goal is for students to "think like content area 'insiders'" (Buehl, 2009b, p. 229). Literacy support for secondary teachers often seems problematic and misaligned with the needs of content teachers in terms of curricula and schedules. Teachers voice the need for relevant, applicable, and effective professional support as they guide their students in content literacy. It is our hope that you will become encouraged to incorporate this book's strategies, techniques, assessment guides, and teacher talk in content classrooms to sustain our secondary strategic readers.

Chapter 3

Word Study: The Wonder of Words

Synthesizing with **Roll-Read-Record (3Rs)**

Spelling with **Word Sorts**

Synthesizing with **Syllable Juncture**

As we strive to sustain strategic readers, it is necessary to provide educators with a clear understanding of adolescent word study and the value of a word study focus, and to explore which strategies and techniques are vital to implement a solid word study foundation. Middle school and high school teachers face a growing number of students lacking basic proficiency in reading and writing. According to the National Assessment of Educational Progress (2009), only 38% of 12th graders are performing at or above the proficiency level in reading. Through our instructional coaching and professional development, conversations with secondary teachers and other reading educators have expressed a need to emphasize word study within content instruction.

Content teachers can effectively infuse word study techniques within daily classroom instruction (Berne & Blachowicz, 2008; Bloodgood & Pacifici, 2004; Hennings, 2000). An essential component of vocabulary learning and acquisition is word study, involving more than memorizing individual vocabulary definitions. Word study guides students' attention to the letter–sound combinations, meaning and structure of words, spelling patterns, and morphemic analysis (i.e., prefixes, suffixes, roots) needed to move beyond literal acquisition into comparison, analysis, and synthesis level of deriving meaning. The goals are to support secondary readers in understanding derivational patterns in content vocabulary and to support educators in applying orthographic knowledge as a foundation to build higher level reading and writing (Bloodgood & Pacifici, 2004; Harris, 2007).

An analysis of the impact on reading comprehension indicates a correlation between a greater understanding of morphology, the study of word structure, and higher comprehension scores. Adolescent readers use the foundation of known words to manipulate word parts and increase recognition, and they use these models or analogies to identify similar patterns in other content vocabulary (Bhattacharya & Ehri, 2004; Kieffer & Lesaux, 2007; Lesaux & Kieffer, 2010). To effectively use the word study strategies and techniques presented in this chapter, ample time should be allotted for teacher modeling, student engagement, and scaffolding of learning. The goal is to structure instruction to support independent application and student ownership of learning.

Teachers can use the Motivation/Engagement section within many techniques as an additional means of motivating the whole learner and creating 21st-century secondary learners (refer to Chapter 1 for a description of *whole learner* and to Figure 1.1 for an illustration of a 21st-century secondary learner). The Motivation/Engagement section allows for differentiation within the technique as needed to meet the needs of all learners. This section identifies and uses a multiple intelligence other than those that are highlighted in the main procedure of the technique.

Educators should use the word study strategies and techniques within the lesson planning and instructional process. However, it is essential to understand that these strategies and techniques are multifaceted and can be interchangeable within the components of lesson planning (before, during, and after instruction). These word study techniques support secondary readers to sustain independence as readers and acquire the reading strategies.

The following are the strategies and techniques in this chapter:

- Synthesizing: Alliteration Creation, Sounds Abound, Roll-Read-Record (3Rs), Syllable Juncture

- Analyzing Affixes: DISSECT, Four Square Structure, Sufficient Suffixes

- Analyzing Root Words: Wordsmith Work, Realizing Roots, Rappin' With Roots

- Spelling: Mnemonics, Word Sorts, Multi-Sensory Spelling, Incidental Spelling

Word Study Strategy: Synthesizing

Synthesizing emphasizes the structure of the written language and enables readers to recognize words rapidly and seamlessly. The ability to associate *phonemes* (sounds) with represented *graphemes* (letters) and then combine the sounds and letters to form a meaningful word is the foundation for synthetic/inductive phonics. When adolescent readers synthesize, they are fusing the *alphabetic principle* and applying both *decoding* skills for reading and *encoding* skills for writing. Research estimates that 10% of adolescent readers struggle to decode (Biancarosa & Snow, 2006; Kamil, 2003; National Association of State Boards of Education, 2006). Word study for these learners needs to be both explicit and implicit in the instructional approach to allow for successful secondary readers to move to a *metalinguistic* level. As readers think about the articulation of specific sounds, they are able to focus on the separate distinctions of the sound parts within words to form a whole word. There is also evidence that "the more students pay attention to what their mouths do when they make a speech sound, the more likely they are to remember the association of sound to letter" (Herron, 2008, p. 80).

Key Vocabulary for Synthesizing

- Alphabetic Principle: decoding print to speech or oral language
- Decoding: process of translating a printed word into sounds by using knowledge of the conventions of letter–sound relationships and knowledge about pronunciation of irregular words to derive a pronunciation of written words; applying graphemes to phonemes, syllables, or morphemes
- Encoding: spelling; listening for sounds and deciding on the letters that represent the phonemes
- Grapheme: the written symbol (i.e., letter) used to represent a phoneme
- Metalinguistic: related to the ability to think about and reflect on one's language
- Phoneme: the smallest segment of sound used to form a word

Assessment for Synthesizing

Use the following behaviors as a guide as you assess students' abilities to synthesize. Do students exhibit these behaviors never, rarely, often, or always?

- ☐ Translates print into speech by corresponding graphemes to phonemes (letters to sounds) when reading orally
- ☐ Breaks words into parts (e.g., compound words, root) and combines word parts to create words
- ☐ Listens to sounds and identifies letters that represent the sounds (e.g., when the teacher says "pre," the student responds with the letter names "p-r-e")

Teacher Talk: Statements, Questions, and Prompts for Synthesizing

The following are suggestions for teacher talk that encourages readers to think strategically as they employ the synthesizing strategy. Try using some of these statements, questions, and prompts with your students as you work through the techniques in the following section. They are aligned with Bloom's taxonomy and Webb's DOK levels.

Level of Thinking	Teacher Talk
Creating Extended Thinking	• Reflect on the benefits of using alliteration. How do you apply alliteration as a memory device and even as a study skill for assessments?
	• Think about how words are broken into syllables as you listen to this word aloud. Explain the steps you used to determine your process for dividing the word.
Evaluating Strategic Thinking	• Select several words and compare and contrast the individual sounds within the words. Explain why each word is categorized.
Analyzing Strategic Thinking	• Using a comprehension question relating to specific content, create your response to the question in an alliteration format.
	• When you stretch the word, what is happening?
Applying Skill/Concept	• Think of words that begin with the same sound as _____. What other words start the same as _____ and can create an alliterative jingle?
	• Identify the sounds you hear in the word _____.
Understanding Skill/Concept	• Think about this word and how the sounds and letters are associated.
	• How does hearing the sounds slowly help you form a word?
	• Describe why these sounds are connected.
Remembering Recall	• What word do you form when you blend these letters?
	• How many sounds do you hear in the word _____?
	• Listen to the sentence and position your mouth to represent the repeated sounds you hear. Describe the position of your mouth for that sound.

Alliteration Creation

Alliteration Creation in the Classroom:

An 11th-grade English literature teacher used "The Raven" by Edgar Allan Poe with his students to highlight alliteration. After reading the following example of alliteration from the poem, students were asked to craft their own alliteration creations.

> Deep into that darkness peering, long I stood there wondering, fearing/ Doubting, dreaming dreams no mortal ever dared to dream before

Purpose: To identify and apply the repetition of initial consonants of words

Multiple Intelligences: Visual/spatial, verbal/linguistic, logical/mathematical, interpersonal, intrapersonal

Materials: Poetry, jingles, song lyrics, other text examples of alliteration, student journals, chart paper, and content text (mirrors); Optional: student laptops

Procedure:

1. Facilitate a discussion, with examples, of the concept of alliteration (repetition of sounds at the beginning of words).

2. Ask students to recite and demonstrate tongue twisters using alliteration.

Suggested Teacher Talk: *Think of words that begin with the same sound as _____. What other words start the same as _____ and can create an alliterative jingle?*

3. Select passages from poetry, content text, song lyrics, or other literacy texts that are appropriate examples of alliteration. Read aloud the excerpts, facilitating discussion on the repeated sound and how this literary style creates a unique meaning and rhyme in the text.

4. Have students work independently or with a partner to create their own poetry or prose using alliteration. Encourage students to share their alliteration creations aloud.

Suggested Teacher Talk: *Reflect on the benefits of using alliteration. How do you apply alliteration as a memory device and even as a study skill for assessments?*

5. Explore text pieces from various content areas for examples of alliteration.

Suggested Teacher Talk: *Using a comprehension question relating to specific content, create your response to the question in an alliterative format. For example, for social studies content you might write, "Responding, Roosevelt revealed his relevant plan for revamping the allied resources."*

Motivation/Engagement: *Bodily/kinesthetic.* After students read their alliteration creations, have partners isolate the repeated sounds by using a handheld mirror to demonstrate the positioning of the sound. In pairs, students describe to each other what they notice happening to their mouths when they repeat the alliteration.

Suggested Teacher Talk: *Listen to the sentence and position your mouth to represent the repeated sounds you hear. Describe the position of your mouth for that sound.*

Sounds Abound

Purpose: To isolate, identify, and match beginning and ending sounds in content area vocabulary

Multiple Intelligences: Verbal/linguistic, interpersonal

Materials: Starter word, content text, literature, vocabulary journal, timer, chart paper

Procedure:

1. After a content area lesson, form small groups of students—"sound" teams—to create a Sounds Abound (Ellery, 2009; Zgonc, 1999) list. Have the teams select a recorder to capture their vocabulary Sounds Abound list. The list consists of words that relate to the given concept or content, where each word is connected by the ending sound of one word becoming the beginning sound of the next word.

2. Set a timer for approximately five minutes. Provide the students on the sound team with a starter word or content area concept (e.g., algebraic sets).

Suggested Teacher Talk: *Think about the chosen concept and vocabulary words that relate to it. Create a list of words that can be linked together by their beginning and ending sounds and that relate to the concept. What sound do you hear at the end of the word _____? Now, try to think of a word that begins with that sound to add to your team list from the related topic.*

3. Students take turns thinking of a word that begins with the ending sound of the last word created (e.g., algebraic sets: *difference, set, transitive, Venn, null, laws, subset, transitivity, equality*; see Figure 3.1 for more examples of Sounds Abound lists using vocabulary for different content areas). Discuss how the final sound, not the final letter, is used when coming up with a new word (e.g., in *difference*, /s/ is the final sound, not the sound for *e*).

FIGURE 3.1. Example Sounds Abound Lists for Various Content Areas

Content Area	Target Word or Concept	Sounds Abound List
Science	endangered sea turtle	turtle, lost, tumor, recovery, evolve, vision, nest, transport
Literature	Beowulf	Beowulf, funeral, last, transcription, ninth hour, remains, Scandinavia, alliterative
Mathematics	algebraic sets	equation, notation, null, linear, roots, solve, variable

4. After time has expired, have teams reflect on their list of content vocabulary and determine if the beginning and ending sounds align properly, as well as whether the meaning of the words relates to the content.

Motivation/Engagement: *Visual/spatial.* Have students share to the whole group and chart team lists into categories depending on content (e.g., literary elements, categories of living things).

Roll-Read-Record (3Rs)

Purpose: To hear sounds within words, associate a letter or letters with the sounds, and then blend sounds together to form words

Multiple Intelligences: Visual/spatial, verbal/linguistic, bodily/kinesthetic, interpersonal

Materials: Roll-Read-Record Graphing Chart reproducible (see Appendix), content-specific text, large and small number cubes (i.e., dice)

Procedure:

1. *Roll*: After reading an excerpt of content-specific text, partners roll a number cube and then search for a word within the text that has the same number of sounds (phonemes) or syllables as the number on the cube.

2. *Read*: One student reads the selected word slowly while the partner listens to the sound parts in the chosen word.

3. *Record*: Once the sounds parts have been isolated and the number of sounds or syllables determined, the students record the word on their graphing chart.

Motivation/Engagement: *Logical/mathematical.* Students work with partners to roll, read, and record (Ellery, 2009) their vocabulary or spelling words and justify why they placed their words under the specific columns. Students can search online for content-specific vocabulary and apply the 3Rs as they process the information.

Suggested Teacher Talk: *Select several words and compare and contrast the individual sounds within the words. Explain why each word is categorized.*

Syllable Juncture

Purpose: To determine word meaning for abstract concepts by combining frequently used roots and affixes

Multiple Intelligences: Visual/spatial, verbal/linguistic, bodily/kinesthetic, interpersonal

Materials: Note cards or sticky notes, print or online content text or both, chart paper, visual projection device

Procedure:

1. Review common guidelines for counting syllables and dividing words into syllables:

    Counting Syllables

    a. Count the vowels in the word (e.g., *outside* has four vowels).

    b. Subtract any silent vowels. For example, subtract the silent *e* at the end of a word, or the second vowel when two vowels are together in a syllable (e.g., *outside*: four vowels minus one silent *e* equals three vowels).

    c. Subtract one vowel from every diphthong (e.g., *ou* counts only as one vowel sound, so *outside* now has two vowels).

    d. Count the number of vowel sounds left, and it will equal the number of syllables in the word (e.g., *outside* has two syllables because it has two remaining vowels).

    e. Check the number of syllables that you hear when you pronounce a word against the number of vowels sounds heard (e.g., the word *outside* has four vowels, but the *e* is silent and the *ou* is a diphthong, so this word has two syllables).

    Dividing Words Into Syllables

    a. Divide syllables between two middle consonants (e.g., *mid/dle*). Exceptions to this rule are digraphs (e.g., *th*, *wh*, *ch*, *sh*, and *ph*), which represent one sound and are never split.

    b. Divide after the consonant that precedes an *le* syllable (e.g., *tumb/le*).

    c. Divide any compound words and affixes that contain vowels (e.g., *pre/test*, *down/town*, *teach/er*).

    d. Usually divide before a single middle consonant (*o/pen*).

2. Select content words relating to the current unit of study. Read the words aloud and have the students listen to the words, examine sounds, and determine how many syllables are in each word using the previous steps and guidelines for support.

3. Model the Syllable Juncture process using note cards or sticky notes to denote each syllable in the example word.

Suggested Teacher Talk: *Think about how words are broken into syllables as you listen to this word aloud. Explain the steps you used to determine your process for dividing the word.*

4. Students can work in small groups or pairs to self-select vocabulary words from print or online text and create their own Syllable Juncture cards (e.g., *aer/o/dy/nam/ics*).

5. Encourage groups to present their content vocabulary words. Capture the class list on a chart and reflect on the meanings of the words within the content. Use this process to reinforce use of the syllabication guidelines and spelling patterns and as a preview or review of key content vocabulary.

Motivation/Engagement: *Logical/mathematical.* Display a list of 15 to 20 key vocabulary words from the content text or topic. Students write one word per note card and use the cards to play various word games like Word Study Uno or Syllable Rummy (Johnston, Invernizzi, Bear, & Templeton, 2009). Students match cards based on the number of syllables in each word.

Word Study Strategy: Analyzing Affixes

When students analyze prefixes and suffixes, they implicitly discover the intricacies of word power. Analyzing the structure, or word parts, is a way to determine the meaning of a word because it involves examining *affixes* (i.e., prefixes, suffixes) attached to base words. Studying the *morphemes* (i.e., the smallest meaningful unit in a word) allows students to acquire information about the meaning, phonological representation, and word parts of new words (Nagy, Diakidoy, & Anderson, 1991). These word parts contribute to the meaning of the word through *morphemic analysis* (Ebbers & Denton, 2008). When adolescent readers discover a word in their content area vocabulary, they can investigate its parts to obtain meaning, because "approximately 80% of words in the English dictionary contain Greek or Latin prefixes, suffixes, or roots" (Manzo & Manzo, 2008, p. 97).

Key Vocabulary for Analyzing Affixes

- Affix: a morpheme attached to a base word to form a new word
- Morpheme: the smallest meaningful linguistic unit in a word (e.g., prefixes, suffixes, inflectional endings)
- Morphemic Analysis: the process of analyzing the grammatical structure of a word, sentence, or both

Assessment for Analyzing Affixes

Use the following behaviors as a guide as you assess students' abilities to analyze affixes. Do students exhibit these behaviors never, rarely, often, or always?

☐ Locates affixes in words and examines their meanings

☐ Deciphers the structure of new words (e.g., affixes, inflections) to derive word meaning

☐ Analyzes visual patterns to determine how word meaning may change as a result of adding prefixes, suffixes, or both to the root word

Teacher Talk: Statements, Questions, and Prompts for Analyzing Affixes

The following are suggestions for teacher talk that encourages readers to think strategically as they employ the analyzing affixes strategy. Try using some of these statements, questions, and prompts with your students as you work through the techniques in the following section. They are aligned with Bloom's taxonomy and Webb's DOK levels.

Level of Thinking	Teacher Talk
Creating Extended Thinking	• What does the prefix _____ do when added to the start of the word _____? What words go with this word? • Think about the content area of study. Reflect on the upper left quadrant on your Four Square Structure and describe the meaning of the word part. How does the affix modify the meaning of the word and solidify the content meaning?
Evaluating Strategic Thinking	• Describe how studying the affix within the word helps you. • What questions did you ask yourself that helped you to figure out the meaning of unknown word?
Analyzing Strategic Thinking	• Look at your words and think about how the words are designed. How are all these words alike? • Think about the word parts presented. How does the analysis of the affixes help to determine word meaning?
Applying Skill/Concept	• Look for any parts of a word that help you to make sense of it. Take the word apart. • How does the affix modify the meaning of each word?
Understanding Skill/Concept	• What is the meaning of the prefix or suffix? How do the words relate in meaning?
Remembering Recall	• Identify the prefix or suffix within the word. Which word has a prefix? Which word has a suffix?

Techniques for Analyzing Affixes

DISSECT

Purpose: To examine multisyllabic content vocabulary to bring meaning to the whole word

Multiple Intelligences: Visual/spatial, verbal/linguistic, logical/mathematical, interpersonal

Materials: DISSECT reproducible (see Appendix), text; Optional: dictionary

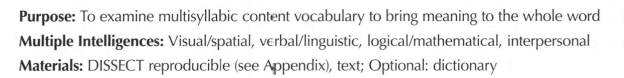

Word Study: Analyzing Affixes

Procedure:

1. Have students DISSECT (Deshler & Schumaker, 1988; Ellery, 2009; Lenz & Hughes, 1990) words from content area text step by step.

   - *Discover the context* by examining syntactic and semantic cues when reading. As students approach an unknown word, they skip the word and read to the end of the sentence. Then, using the context of the sentence, they make a logical guess about the unknown word's meaning.

   - *Isolate the prefix* by separating it from the root. Students look at the first part of the word and try to pronounce the sequence of letters. If a prefix is identified, students can draw a box around it to isolate the prefix.

   - *Separate the suffix* by dividing it from the root. Students look at the end of the word to determine if they can draw a box or separate the ending letters.

   - *Say the stem* by attempting to pronounce what is left of the word. If the stem is recognized, students can read the prefix, stem, and suffix together. If the root is not recognized, have the students continue to dissect the word by examining the stem.

   - *Examine the stem* by dividing the letters and applying phonetic knowledge. Example phonetic generalizations: If the stem or part of the stem begins with a vowel, separate the first two letters; if it begins with a consonant, separate the first three letters and pronounce. Students follow through until the stem is reached. If the students still cannot make sense of the stem, they take off the first letter of the stem and try again. The students can check the hints for pronunciation when two different vowels are together.

   - *Check with someone.* If students are unable to read the unknown word after the first five steps, they should ask someone else for ideas,

   or

   - *Try another resource,* such as a dictionary, to identify the word. Students should use the pronunciation guide to try to pronounce the word and read the definition to determine meaning of the word.

   Suggested Teacher Talk: *Explain the generalization you see in the word. How does studying the word help you?*

2. After students record their findings on the DISSECT reproducible, ask them to work with a partner and share their discovery.

Motivation/Engagement: *Bodily/kinesthetic.* Discuss the concept of dissecting an object or animal to examine its parts. Have the students practice dissecting several words into pronounceable word parts. They can record their findings in learning logs and justify any phonetic generalizations that they note. Although secondary strategic readers do not necessarily consult rules when reading, knowing the generalizations can help them analyze words and compare an unknown word to known words with similarities.

Four Square Structure

Purpose: To analyze visual patterns to determine how word meaning may change as a result of adding prefixes, suffixes, or both

Multiple Intelligences: Visual/spatial, verbal/linguistic, logical/mathematical, interpersonal, intrapersonal

Materials: Content text, multipurpose paper or notebook paper, markers, highlighters, print or online dictionary or both, content vocabulary with root words, prefixes, and suffixes

Procedure:

1. Select content area vocabulary from the topic of study or text selection, identifying terms that have a similar root word, prefix, or suffix. Model a sample by using a visual projection device or chart to highlight Four Square Structure.

2. Ask students to fold a blank sheet of notebook or printer paper into four equal sections. Have students write the target word in the upper left quadrant, the affix or root word in the upper right quadrant with its meaning, a context or student-friendly definition in the lower left quadrant, and list three or four other example words that have a similar patterns (prefix, suffix, root word) in the lower right quadrant (Hedrick, Harmon, & Wood, 2008; Stahl & Nagy, 2006; see Figure 3.2 for an example).

3. Students examine the meaning and function of the word in the specific content area based on the entire Four Square Structure of the word.

Suggested Teacher Talk: *Think about the content area of study. Reflect on the upper left quadrant on your four square structure and describe the meaning of the word part. How does the affix modify the meaning of the word and solidify the content meaning?*

4. Have students reflect on how the affix modifies the meaning of the root word.

5. Explore content text pieces for other academic vocabulary that contain root words, prefixes, or suffixes.

Motivation/Engagement: *Bodily/kinesthetic.* Use "if-then" statements to describe the connection between root word meaning and modifications in context when using affixes (e.g., If *reliable* means dependable, then *reliability* means the ability to be reliant or

FIGURE 3.2. Example of the Four Square Structure for a Social Studies Vocabulary Word

Content Word recondition	Affix Meaning Prefix re- = again "To fix or condition again"
Content-Related Sentence The history club volunteered to help recondition the old train engine.	Additional Examples resurface revisit remodel

trustworthy). Create a four square setting for students to participate in "Four Square" by bouncing a ball into each quadrant and answering with the appropriate response.

Sufficient Suffixes

Purpose: To add suffixes to change a word to a different part of speech

Multiple Intelligences: Visual/spatial, verbal/linguistic, interpersonal, intrapersonal

Materials: Common Content Area Roots and Affixes reproducible (see Appendix), vocabulary notebooks or journals

Procedure:

1. Choose possible suffixes to change nouns to verbs, verbs to nouns or adjectives, and adjectives to nouns. Review the content-specific examples of nouns, verbs, and adjectives, modeling how to use the list of suffixes to change the word to a different part of speech.

2. Students work with a partner to select a noun, verb, or adjective from the word list and add appropriate suffixes to change the word to a different part of speech.

3. Students record their list of words, suffixes, and the newly generated words (see Figure 3.3 for an example).

4. Facilitate a group share of newly generated words and record the words on chart paper, a whiteboard, or a classroom word wall.

Suggested Teacher Talk: *Think about the word parts presented. How does the analysis of the affixes help to determine word meaning?*

5. Refer students to content-specific text and note additional words with similar suffixes.

Motivation/Engagement: *Logical/mathematical.* Challenge students to think of additional nouns, verbs, adjectives, and suffixes and to generate new words with them. Students use a print or online dictionary to check spelling and the part of speech of the new vocabulary.

FIGURE 3.3. Examples of Modifying Sufficient Suffixes

Original Word	Suffix Added	New Word Created	Part of Speech Formed
patriot	ism	patriotism	noun
real	ist	realist	noun
bounty	ful	bountiful	adjective
vary	able	variable	noun or adjective
equate	ation	equation	noun
blind	ness	blindness	noun
measure	ment	measurement	noun

Students use vocabulary relevant to the current theme or topic, identify the part of speech, and analyze how adding a suffix might modify the meaning of the word.

Word Study Strategy: Analyzing Root Words

According to Berne and Blachowicz (2008), "Decoding skills, fluency skills, and comprehension skills all draw upon a known bank of words" (p. 315). Many words used in content area learning derive meaning from *root words* that may represent the same meaning in varied content areas. "By emphasizing these meaningful word parts, teachers help students develop a powerful, independent learning strategy that is transferable to many word learning opportunities" (Harmon, Wood, & Hedrick, 2006, p. 107). These small units of language can stand alone (e.g., *graph* and *photo*) or derive meaning when attached to other word parts (e.g., *ing*, *ed*, or *micro*). Students are led to recognize clusters of similar words with common roots and can acquire understanding of other related content vocabulary when they use *morphemic analysis* and *structural analysis* (Ebbers & Denton, 2008). "Once words are broken into parts, students can use their knowledge of word parts to attempt to deduce their meaning—if they understand how word parts function" (Graves, 2006, p.103).

Key Vocabulary for Analyzing Root Words

- Morphemic Analysis: the process of analyzing the grammatical structure of words and sentences

- Root Word: the form of a word that contains the basic meaning of the word after the affixes are removed; base element; stem; can form a whole word by itself

- Structural Analysis: the study of the word parts to derive meaning of a word

Assessment for Analyzing Root Words

Use the following behaviors as a guide as you assess students' abilities to analyze root words. Do students exhibit these behaviors never, rarely, often, or always?

- ☐ Locates the root of the word and examines its meaning

- ☐ Deciphers the structure of base words to derive word meaning

- ☐ Applies affixes to derive conceptual knowledge of vocabulary with similar base word patterns

Teacher Talk: Statements, Questions, and Prompts for Analyzing Root Words

The following are suggestions for teacher talk that encourages readers to think strategically as they employ the analyzing root words strategy. Try using some of these statements, questions, and prompts with your students as you work through the techniques in the following section. They are aligned with Bloom's taxonomy and Webb's DOK levels.

Level of Thinking	Teacher Talk
Creating 　Extended Thinking	• If you know what the root word for _____ means, what do you think _____ means? Describe why you connected these word parts. Explain how these words relate and can be categorized.
Evaluating 　Strategic Thinking	• How does knowing the history of the word make it more memorable and support you? • Describe how studying the root word within the word helps you. • What questions did you ask yourself that helped you to figure out the meaning of the unknown word through root word analysis?
Analyzing 　Strategic Thinking	• Analyze the foundational part of the word and determine the origin of the word. • How do root words compare and contrast across content areas?
Applying 　Skill/Concept	• What prefixes or suffixes can you add to the base word to create a new word?
Understanding 　Skill/Concept	• What is the root word of _____? What does it mean?
Remembering 　Recall	• Define the meaning of a root word. • What is a prefix or suffix?

Techniques for Analyzing Root Words

Wordsmith Work

Purpose: To recognize and use known root words and affixes to derive conceptual knowledge of additional academic vocabulary with similar base word patterns

Multiple Intelligences: Visual/spatial, verbal/linguistic, interpersonal, intrapersonal

Materials: Common Content Roots and Affixes reproducible (see Appendix), content text, print or online dictionary or both, highlighter, student journals or vocabulary notebooks, list of familiar or previously taught root words

Procedure:

1. Have students use online or print dictionaries to research the meaning of each word in the context of the topic they are studying.

(Example content words: social studies—*chrono* [time], *cracy/crat* [government], *socio* [society], *nom* [order/management]; science—*cosmo* [universe], *still* [star], *therm* [heat], sect [cut], *phyte* [plant]; math—*equi* [equal/same], *sect* [cut], *gon* [angle], *lateral* [side], *tract* [draw])

Suggested Teacher Talk: *Think about the word parts presented. How does the analysis of the affixes help to determine word meaning?*

2. Have students compare and contrast their root word meanings with a partner. In a shared setting, partners report to the whole group the meaning for a common understanding of each root word.

3. Model the process for generating new words by manipulating affixes (prefixes or suffixes) and root words (also known as base or stem words) to generate new words. Ask the students to be "wordsmiths" (Padak, Newton, Rasinski, & Newton, 2008, p. 22), using the parts of words to create new words. For example, *demo* + *cracy* = *democracy* or *re* + *tract* = *retract*.

4. Facilitate a group discussion of the created words.

Suggested Teacher Talk: *Describe why you connected these word parts. Explain how these words relate and can be categorized.*

Motivation/Engagement: *Logical/mathematical.* Have students refer to content text and note or highlight words with similar root structures. Encourage students to work independently or with a partner to predict possible definitions and examine their print or online dictionaries to research the definition for each of the words they have generated.

Realizing Roots

Realizing Roots in the Classroom:

Sue Darovec, a middle school language arts teacher, supports her students in making connections between the use of affixes in familiar words and unfamiliar words. Mrs. Darovec specifies an affix and encourages her students to brainstorm words that begin or end with it. Her class forms teams, and they are challenged to identify additional words that correctly contain the affix. Each team sends one student to write an example on the classroom interactive whiteboard. Team members take turns adding words. This activity continues until each team has identified 8 to 10 words that are examples for the specific affix. Each team creates a prefix chart, which is a graphic organizer for the affixes and examples listed on the interactive whiteboard. This chart consists of a single sheet of paper folded into quarters lengthwise, whose columns are labeled *Affix, Example Word 1, Example Word 2,* and *Meaning.* Teams or individual students choose two example words that use the affix accurately.

Affix	Example Word 1	Example Word 2	Meaning

Purpose: To derive meaning from a root word, also known as the stem or base word

Multiple Intelligences: Visual/spatial, verbal/linguistic, logical/mathematical, interpersonal, intrapersonal

Materials: Content area texts, computers with Internet access, dictionaries, journals, highlighters

Procedure:

1. Ask students to listen to the following passage and reflect on the meaning of the term *root*.

Learning the *root* of a word can help derive the meaning. Sixty percent of all English words have a Latin or Greek origin; therefore, many of our *root* words have a base element or basic meaning derived from a language other than English. The word *root* also is used in fields other than the study of language, such as dentistry, mathematics, and botany. Discuss how the *roots* of language study can be compared with *roots* in other fields or content areas.

2. *Discuss:* Share reactions to the term *root* and how it relates to the study of language.

3. *Define:* Divide the students into teams and give each team a root word on an index card. Teams research the meaning and origin of the root word and record a story or history of the word. They can use dictionaries or the Internet for resources.

Suggested Teacher Talk: *Analyze the foundational part of the word and determine the origin of the word. How does knowing the history of the word make it more memorable and support you?*

4. *Detail:* Students generate a set of new words by adding affixes (prefixes and suffixes) to the root words and then record new words in a journal. Have students explore their content area reading to locate words that relate to their root word in context.

Suggested Teacher Talk: *What is the root of the word _____? What prefixes or suffixes can you add to the base word to create a new word?*

5. *Design:* Students draw or add visuals, diagrams, or pictures to support their words. Once original words are created from combining several root words, students are encouraged to create a sentence using the newly created word in context.

6. *Deliver:* Teams share their findings with whole group.

Rappin' With Roots

Purpose: To determine the meaning of abstract concepts by combining frequently used roots and affixes

Multiple Intelligences: Visual/spatial, verbal/linguistic, musical/rhythmic, interpersonal

Materials: Word Root Tree (see Appendix), note cards or sticky notes, print or online content text or both, chart paper, visual projection device

Procedure: Use a variety of word games, rhythm, and rhyme to reinforce the meaning of roots and affixes and how they can be used to decipher content word meaning. Instruction focusing on common roots and affixes can support students in comprehending content text, using context clues, and improving spelling skills.

1. Words Within Words: Use note cards or sticky notes for students to create word cards. Each student researches and records a content definition, example, or both and teaches the term to a partner or small group. On one side of the card the student writes the key term and on the other the context definition, identifying the meanings of roots and affixes (e.g., *epidermis*: *epi-* [on, around] + *dermis* [skin covering] = layer of skin covering). Encourage the students to use nonlinguistic representations to clarify their word descriptions. Students can share their Words Within Words cards with a partner.

2. Root/Affix Concentration: Students use content vocabulary words that contain affixes to create their own Root/Affix Concentration game. The root word can be written on one note card and possible affixes on another card. Students work with a partner to select two cards and determine if they are a "match." A match would be an affix and root word that create an appropriate content vocabulary word. Another application of Root/Affix Concentration is to write the affix on one card and the meaning on the other (e.g., *pre* on one card and *before* on another). Determine if cards match by showing an affix and its meaning. If there is a match, pick up the cards and place them to the side. If cards do not match, return them to their original positions.

3. Circle Roots: Students craft their own Circle Roots (adapted from Harmon et al., 2006; Vacca & Vacca, 2008) and are encouraged to think critically about the relationships between roots and affixes. Students divide a circle into quarters and write a word in each section. Students can then orally or in print identify and describe the relationship that exists among the words. For example, the selected term may be *prescribe*, and other terms containing the root word *scribe* include *describe*, *inscribe*, and *subscribe* (see Figure 3.4).

FIGURE 3.4. Circle Roots

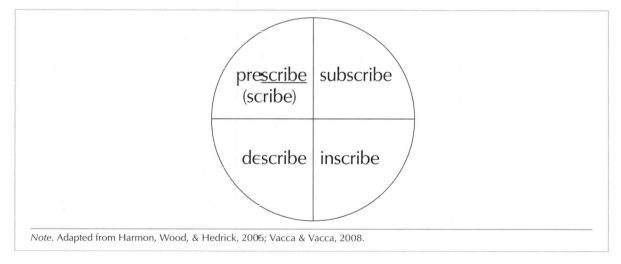

Note. Adapted from Harmon, Wood, & Hedrick, 2006; Vacca & Vacca, 2008.

Suggested Teacher Talk: *How do the four words relate in meaning? How does the affix modify the meaning of each word?*

4. Rhythm Roots: Students create a lyrical rap to describe the meanings and purposes of Latin and Greek roots and affixes. Examples are available online at www.educationalrap .com. The following is one example (reprinted here with permission):

> Words are power and that's the truth
> Prefixes, suffixes, and they all got roots
> Words are power, they run this town
> So let's run the track and break 'em down!

Motivation/Engagement: *Logical/mathematical.* Use the Word Root Tree (see Appendix) as a note-taking guide for common content-specific roots, affixes, and sample words. Students can maintain their Word Root Tree notes in student notebooks or journals.

Word Study Strategy: Spelling

Spelling is a strategy that allows the reader to transform sounds into letters and letters into written words. As students read, they create a visual imprint of the written shape of the words, identifying patterns within words, and exploring the use of the word in context as it is spelled. "Learning to spell *English* is a developmental exploration of this balance between sound and meaning in which learners move from the expectation that spelling represents sound to the understanding that spelling also represents meaning" (Templeton, 2003, p. 738). Students can compare parts of an unknown word with similar parts of a known word to form the spelling of the word using the *analogy approach* to phonetics (National Institute of Child Health and Human Development, 2000; White, 2005). They may also use a *mnemonic* approach to assist in recall. Instruction in spelling explicitly allows readers to transfer word knowledge successfully into their independent writing (Amtmann, Abbott, & Berninger, 2008).

Adolescents demonstrate cognitive process by advancing through developmental spelling stages to become strategic conventional spellers, indicating their ability to grasp the vital understanding of *orthography*. Inspecting, visualizing, chunking, sounding out, approximating, patterning, using memory devices, and recognizing are all ways to gain command with word and orthographic knowledge. Students who apply these spelling components are able to identify words automatically in a cognitive process. There are numerous studies that demonstrate the orthographic stages and spelling inventories for determining students' characteristics to gain *word power* (Bear, Invernizzi, Templeton, & Johnston, 2008; Sharp, Sinatra, & Reynolds, 2008; Viise, 1996). A representation of these spelling acquisition stages is found in Table 3.1. Secondary spellers operate mainly in Stage IV (Syllables and Affixes), and Stage V (*Derivational Relations*) as they begin to shift toward content area reading.

TABLE 3.1. Spelling Acquisition Stages

Spelling Acquisition Stages	Grade Range	Stage Indicators
Stage III Patterns Within Words	1–5	• silent *e* • long vowel patterns • *r*-controlled vowels • single syllable words • more complex consonant patterns • dipthongs (*oi, ou, ow*) • homographs and homophones
Stage IV Syllables and Affixes	3–9	• works with word endings and patterns • inflectional endings (*-es, -ed, -ing*) • syllabication • stress and accents in multisyllable words
Stage V Derivational Relations	5–12	• spelling/meaning connections • consonant and vowel alternatives (*native, national*) • word origins (Latin and Greek affixes and root words)

Key Vocabulary for Spelling

- Analogy Approach: a method for decoding in which students access the parts of the word they already know by focusing on spelling patterns like word families

- Derivational Relations: a higher order stage of spelling focusing on morphology (i.e., affixes and roots) of written words

- Mnemonic: an aid to assist memory by linking to prior knowledge or breaking complicated information into more manageable parts or both

- Orthography: the method of representing the spoken language with written symbols; using the correct sequencing of letters in the language writing system

- Word Power: the ability to exercise and communicate meaning of a sound or a combination of a sounds, or its representation in writing or printing

Assessment for Spelling

Use the following behaviors as a guide as you assess students' abilities to spell. Do students exhibit these behaviors never, rarely, often, or always?

- ☐ Develops new words with similar spelling patterns (words within words)

- ☐ Employs the structural elements in their writing of a word (syllables and affixes)

- ☐ Identifies the derivational relations of a word (bases and roots and origin of polysyllabic words)

Teacher Talk: Statements, Questions, and Prompts for Spelling

The following are suggestions for teacher talk that encourages readers to think strategically as they employ the spelling strategy. Try using some of these statements, questions, and prompts with your students as you work through the techniques in the following section. They are aligned with Bloom's taxonomy and Webb's DOK levels.

Level of Thinking	Teacher Talk
Creating Extended Thinking	• What words can you make from these letters? • What is the secret word that uses all of these letters? • Compare this word to other words you know. • What categories would you sort your words into, based on the patterns you see within the words? • Why did you classify these words together?
Evaluating Strategic Thinking	• Determine the origin of the words and examine how knowing this origin supports the spelling of the word. • How does this word fit the pattern in the other words? • How did sorting words or determining categories increase your understanding of the text and clarify spelling patterns?
Analyzing Strategic Thinking	• Describe other words that sound almost the same. • How does knowing how to spell _____ help you spell _____? • Think about the pattern these words have. Explain what features of the words are alike. • Is there another word that you know that has that same "chunk" in it? • Demonstrate how knowing that word helps you with this word.
Applying Skill/Concept	• Think about mnemonic tools that you have used. What are some ways you try to "think out" how to spell a word using a type of mnemonic? • If this is _____ (*point and say the word*), what word might this be? Why?
Understanding Skill/Concept	• Explain a rule or generalization you see in these words. • How are these words similar? • Visualize the word in your mind; "take a picture" of it.
Remembering Recall	• Describe what parts of the word are similar. • Try to think about other "chunks" that are within the word to help you.

Mnemonics

Purpose: To assist memory by linking new information with prior knowledge or by applying verbal and visual cues, or both

Multiple Intelligences: Visual/spatial, verbal/linguistic, rhythmic/musical, interpersonal, intrapersonal

Materials: Content area spelling words; Optional: ReadWriteThink.org lesson titled "Discovering Memory: Li-Young Lee's Poem 'Mnemonic' and the Brain"

Procedure:

1. Explain to students how applying mnemonics may help to break a complicated word into more manageable parts.

Suggested Teacher Talk: *Think about mnemonic tools that you have used. For example, identify ways to remember the order of operations in mathematical equations. What are some ways you try to "think out" how to spell a word using a type of mnemonic?*

2. Brainstorm ways to use memory aids to spell words. Ideas include the following:

   - Word within word

   - Rhymes, rhythmic patterns, or tunes

   - Poetry or exaggerated stories

   - Humorous expressions or personal sayings

   - Keyword encoding, visual representations, or images

   - Acronyms, acrostics, or lists

3. Students target a word from their content area and create one unique mnemonic aid for spelling (see Figure 3.5 for examples using vocabulary from different content areas). Students create associations to remember the proper spelling of targeted words.

Suggested Teacher Talk: *Justify how you have organized the letters so that you can remember the word most effectively.*

4. Students share their mnemonic tricks with partners and record each other's ideas in a word journal.

Motivation/Engagement: *Logical/mathematical.* Create a lesson on the brain using "Discovering Memory: Li-Young Lee's Poem 'Mnemonic' and the Brain," from www.readwritethink.org.

FIGURE 3.5. Examples of Mnemonics Across Content Areas

Content Area	Vocabulary Word	Mnemonic	Type of Memory Aid
Mathematics	perimeter	small word "rim" rim = outside edge sum of the sides	word within word
Language	separate	There once was a farmer named Sep, and one day his wife saw a rat. She yelled, "Sep! A rat-E!"	exaggerated story
Social Studies	neighbor	sleigh ride with my neighbor sleigh/neighbor	rhyming
Science	dissect	Divide In Sections So Everyone Can Tell	acronym

Word Sorts

Word Study:
Spelling

Purpose: To actively use background knowledge to sort words and process understanding of text concepts, word patterns, and common roots

Materials: Note cards or sticky notes, print or online content text or both, chart paper, visual projection device

Multiple Intelligences: Visual/spatial, verbal/linguistic, bodily/kinesthetic, interpersonal, intrapersonal

Procedure:

1. Select 15 to 20 content vocabulary words or identify sample vocabulary words and have students work independently or in small groups to self-select additional words. Determine if this process will be an open or closed Word Sort. Students engage in critical thinking as they examine the word structure and meaning of content vocabulary. Explain how Word Sorts can be open (student determine how to categorize the words) or closed (teacher provides categories), which provides opportunities for students to be actively engaged in words (see ReadWriteThink.org lesson entitled "Sort, Hunt, Write: A Weekly Spelling Program").

2. Capture the selected words on note cards or sticky notes, one word per card. Students work independently or in groups to sort their words into predetermined categories (closed sort) or sort the words and determine their own categories (open sort). Words can be categorized multiple ways using various categories, such as similar word structure patterns (root words and affixes), rhyming words, numbers of syllables, or parts of speech.

Suggested Teacher Talk: *Explain the rationale for the groups you created (open sort).*

3. Establish an appropriate time limit for the students to sort and categorize their words (approximately 10 minutes). Encourage individuals or groups to circulate and examine

other students' Word Sort patterns. As students read and discuss the content, they may need to reclassify their words.

Suggested Teacher Talk: *How did sorting words or determining categories or both increase your understanding of the text and clarify spelling patterns?*

4. Debrief the process in a whole-group setting, having students explain how they categorized their words. Chart or list multiple ways to categorize content words.

Motivation/Engagement: *Logical/mathematical.* Encourage students to use the content words within the context of the theme or topic in the form of a poem, short story, riddle, or rap. Students can scan other sources of print and online texts relevant to the topic or theme to identify words with similar patterns for spelling. Have students list other content-related words that can be added to their Word Sort categories.

Multi-Sensory Spelling

Purpose: To use multiple senses to inspect, explore, visualize, sound out, and approximate the spelling of a word

Multiple Intelligences: Visual/spatial, verbal/linguistic, logical/mathematical, musical/rhythmic, bodily/kinesthetic

Materials: Word work journals; Optional: Spelling Inventory Assessment index cards from *Words Their Way: Word Study for Phonics, Vocabulary, and Spelling Instruction* (4th ed.; Bear et al., 2008)

Procedure:

1. Review the difference between individual sounds (phonemes) and syllables in words.

2. Have students use multiple intelligences to investigate spelling words using the following steps for Working With Words (Ellery 2009; Gaskins, Ehri, Cress, O'Hara, & Donnelly, 1996):

   - Verbal/linguistic: Say aloud the word (e.g., *plethora*). Then say it slowly.

   - Bodily/kinesthetic, verbal/linguistic, and musical/rhythmic: Determine the number of individual phonemes (sounds) in the word by tapping it out (e.g., The word *plethora* has six sounds: /p/ /l/ /e/ /th/ /or/ /a/).

   - Visual/spatial: Look at the word and count out the number of letters in the word (e.g., The word *plethora* has the letters p-l-e-t-h-o-r-a. It has eight letters.).

   - Logical/mathematical: Calculate how many letters and how many sounds are in the word and determine if the word will or will not have one sound for each letter (e.g., There are *eight* letters in the word *plethora*, and because it has *six* sounds it *will not* have a sound for each letter.).

- Logical/mathematical: In a word work journal, draw an underline to represent a space for each phoneme in the word. Then place a slash for each syllable segmentation (e.g., *plethora*: _ _ _ / _ _ / _ _ / _).

- Verbal/linguistic and musical/rhythmic: Think about the spelling of the word and determine what letter or letters are to be written on the lines. Record them (e.g., p l e /th or /a). Say the word, breaking at syllables for a rap or rhythm flow (e.g., "ple, th, or, a") and create a movement to represent the parts.

- Logical/mathematical: Investigate the word and share the phonetic structure of the word (e.g., *p* is a consonant, *l* is a consonant, *e* is a short vowel, *th* is a digraph, *or* is an *r*-controlled vowel, *a* is a schwa sound that is an unaccented syllable vowel).

- Logical/mathematical: Compare and contrast the word to other words from text, word work journals, or a word wall (e.g., *plethora* sounds like *chimera*; *plethora* begins like *plenty* and it also means "plenty" or "excess").

3. Students work in pairs to share their words and locate their word in context.

Motivation/Engagement: *Interpersonal.* Use the spelling inventory assessment in *Words Their Way* (Bear et al., 2008) to determine students' spelling development level. Assign students to groups according to their spelling levels and have them use the Working With Words concept and record word work on individual index cards.

Incidental Spelling

Word Study: Spelling

Purpose: To influence word building, deepen vocabulary knowledge, and strengthen spelling skills

Multiple Intelligences: Visual/spatial, verbal/linguistic, bodily/kinesthetic, interpersonal, intrapersonal

Materials: Common Content Area Roots and Affixes reproducible (see Appendix), print or online content text or both, chart paper or student notebooks, print or online dictionary or both, laptops or student computers

Procedure: Incidental Spelling can be integrated effectively within content lessons to support students in making connections to word patterns. Word Jumbles, Spell It Poetry (Athans & Devine, 2010), and Daily Roots and Affixes (adapted from Bloodgood & Pacifici, 2004) are three ways to engage students throughout a variety of content areas.

1. Word Jumbles: Write letters from content vocabulary words scattered or jumbled on a chart, board, or visual projection device. Students explore the morphemes in depth and manipulate the letters to create the content vocabulary word. Have students self-select additional vocabulary words with challenging spelling patterns and create their own Word Jumbles.

Suggested Teacher Talk: *Explain how you reassembled the Word Jumbles. What spelling patterns did your recognize as your reassembled each content word?*

2. Spell It Poetry: Students select a key content vocabulary word containing a root word and affixes and create an acrostic poem. Each poetry line must begin with the letter on that line and must relate to the word. Use adjectives or phrases to describe each term. It is not necessary for the Spell It Poem to rhyme (e.g., *Aviator*: A = adventuresome, V = V speeds, I = instrument landing system, A = air-foil, t = twin engine, O = Orville Wright, R = radar).

3. Daily Roots and Affixes (adapted from Bloodgood & Pacifici, 2004): Develop a word list of vocabulary derived from content-related roots and affixes (see Common Content Area Roots and Affixes in the Appendix). Post a root or affix on the board and have students brainstorm words that contain the same root or affix. Use as an opening-of-class procedure to activate background knowledge or introduce the lesson. Encourage students to capture their words in student notebooks or journals or list them on the board or chart paper for the whole group. Guide the students to form a hypothesis concerning the meaning of the root or affix and the relation to the content. Have students share their words and predictions with a partner.

Suggested Teacher Talk: *How do the similar roots and affix patterns help you spell the word and discover word meanings?*

Motivation/Engagement: *Logical/mathematical.* Use online resources to create word pictures using four or five challenging content words from a content text selection. Words most frequently presented in the text should be more prominently displayed in the word pictures. These word pictures are also called word clouds: "Word clouds reveal the frequencies of the different words that appear in a piece of text" (McNaught & Lam, 2010, p. 630). A sample online resource can be accessed at www.wordles.com.

Chapter 4

Fluency: Finding the Flow

Expressing with **Radio Reading**

Scaffolding and Rereading
with **Partner Reading**

Pacing with **Rate/Record/Reflect**

luency is multidimensional and represents a level of expertise in combining appropriate phrasing and applying prosodic functions (i.e., stress, phrasing, tone) while reading words automatically. Johns and Berglund (2006, 2010) describe reading fluency as an essential component to comprehending reading material. Rasinski and Fawcett (2008) expand on this by describing fluency as the ability to read effortlessly and with expression, and knowing when to speed up or slow down to acquire meaning. Readers also demonstrate proficiency through fluency strategies such as reading accuracy, pacing, rereading, and wide reading. A reader's ability to apply these fluency strategies serves as an indicator for acquisition of reading skills and as an outcome for reading proficiency (Klauda & Guthrie, 2008; Samuels & Farstrup, 2006; Torgesen, Rashotte, & Alexander, 2001).

Fluency is an essential goal for secondary readers, indicating the relationship between fluency and comprehension. Bringing meaning to the text is an important element of fluency, as indicated by Rasinski and Fawcett (2008): "Although studies that demonstrate a correlation between fluency and comprehension do not prove causation, these studies along with others hold the promise that gains in fluency may account for significant gains in comprehension" (p. 158). Middle and high school teachers are recognizing the need for comprehension strategies, as well as reading fluency techniques, to improve their student comprehension and knowledge of academic content. There is a strong correlation between comprehension difficulties and the inability to read fluently, as laborious reading is frustrating and often leads students to avoid reading altogether. Word recognition and reading fluency difficulties are key contributors to 90% of comprehension problems (Rasinski, Homan, & Biggs, 2009). Although caution must be taken in overuse of timed performance, these expectations to increase students' pace have heightened content teachers' awareness of the validity of including fluency strategies in their instruction. However, this awareness does not provide a case for speed reading. Newkirk (2010) points out, "There is great pleasure in downshifting, in slowing down. We can gain some pleasures and meanings no other way" (p. 6). Newkirk further reminds us that we need to savor reading "for enjoying the infinite ways a sentence can unfold—and for returning to passages that sustain and inspire us" (p. 7).

The independent and self-assured reader demonstrates fluency, which can correlate with work completion. The initial step in planning fluency instruction is to select appropriate-level texts in instruction. Attention to the level of text used in the modeling of fluency strategies is critical in aligning text to readers. The fluency techniques presented are most effectively supported within a student's independent or instructional reading levels. Fluency strategies are essential to comprehension and support reading proficiency (Fuchs, Fuchs, Hosp, & Jenkins, 2001; Pinnell et al., 1995; Rasinski, 2006; Samuels & Farstrup, 2006).

To effectively use the fluency strategies and techniques presented in this chapter, ample time should be allotted for teacher modeling, student engagement, and scaffolding of learning. The goal is to structure instruction to support independent application and student ownership of learning.

Teachers can use the Motivation/Engagement section within many techniques as an additional means of motivating the whole learner and creating 21st-century secondary learners (refer to Chapter 1 for a description of the whole learner and to Figure 1.1 for an illustration of the composition of a 21st-century secondary learner). The Motivation/Engagement section allows for differentiation within the technique as needed to meet the needs of all learners. The section identifies and uses a multiple intelligence other than those that are highlighted in the main procedure of the technique.

Educators should use the fluency strategies and techniques within the lesson planning and instructional process. However, it is essential to understand that these strategies and techniques are multifaceted and can be interchangeable within the lesson. The fluency techniques support secondary readers to sustain independence as readers and acquire the reading strategies.

The following are the strategies and techniques in this chapter:

- Phrasing: Chunk-It/Phrased Reading, Slow to Flow, Eye-Voice Span, Pausing Punctuation

- Scaffolding and Rereading: Frontloading, Partner Reading, Integrated Choral Reading

- Expressing: Interpretative Dialogue, Totally Tonality, Radio Reading, Readers Theatre

- Pacing: Rate/Record/Reflect, Beam Reading, Sprints and Stamina, Commercial Programs

- Wide Reading: Volume Reading, Scaffolding, Literary Tours, Content Read-Aloud

Fluency Strategy: Phrasing

Phrasing is demonstrated when a reader sequences several words together grammatically. This grammatical understanding supports the reader's ability to appropriately use syntax (the way words are put together to form phrases and sentences) as a cueing system when reading and to apply *cohesive chunking*. Syntactic cues involve the reader's ability to identify the function of a word (e.g., noun, verb, preposition) and the basic language pattern associated with a group of words. Appropriate phrasal construction, or syntax, of a sentence demonstrates the timing aspect of *prosody*.

When adolescent readers read in a *seamless* manner, they sound like they are holding a conversation as they read aloud to create a *conversational flow*. Their eyes are moving ahead of their voices to capture the essence of the text prior to bringing voice to the print. The *perceptional span* of a fluent reader needs to make shorter *fixations* and have longer *saccades*, which allow generally smooth reading (Drieghe, Pollatsek, Staub, & Rayner, 2008). Fluent readers using the phrasing strategy apply cohesive chunking and move their eyes freely from word to word or phrase to phrase, "so that they perceive a line of text in terms of successively fixated text images" (Martin, 2004, p. 2). Readers who struggle with the ability to phrase speak in a monotone, have little sense of phrase boundaries, fail to attend to punctuation and clauses, and sound choppy when reading orally. Prosody is one of the key indicators to bringing meaning to what is being read.

Key Vocabulary for Phrasing

- Cohesive Chunking: connecting several words to make a meaningful phrase

- Conversational Flow: moving freely from word to word in a relaxed spoken language

- Fixation: the amount of time directing and focusing the eyes to attend to letters or words

- Perceptual Span: the amount of text that is correctly identified during the fixation pause

- Prosody: the ability to read smoothly, with proper phrasing and expression

- Saccade: the jump or movement of the eye from one fixated point to another
- Seamless: perfectly smooth reading

Assessment for Phrasing

Use the following behaviors as a guide as you assess students' abilities to phrase. Do students exhibit these behaviors never, rarely, often, or always?

☐ Demonstrates the value of forward eye movements and shorter fixations

☐ Uses punctuation to support inflections

☐ Reads seamlessly by sequencing words

Teacher Talk: Statements, Questions, and Prompts for Phrasing

The following are suggestions for teacher talk that encourages readers to think strategically as they employ the phrasing strategy. Try using some of these statements, questions, and prompts with your students as you work through the techniques in the following section. They are aligned with Bloom's taxonomy and Webb's DOK levels.

Level of Thinking	Teacher Talk
Creating Extended Thinking	• Explain why grouping the words helps to make sense out of why you are reading.
Evaluating Strategic Thinking	• Describe how attending to the punctuation supports you in bringing meaning to what is being read. • What would happen if you paused after each word?
Analyzing Strategic Thinking	• Listen as I read these sentences aloud. I will read them using two different types of phrasing. (*Read sentences in two ways.*) Explain which reading sounds better to you and why. • Did your punctuation choices alter the meaning of the original text?
Applying Skill/Concept	• Try to "capture" several words at a time with your eyes ahead of your voice. • Read a passage and think about the value of forward eye movement when reading.
Understanding Skill/Concept	• Describe the eye movement you have when you are reading.
Remembering Recall	• What words are in you holding in your mind that you are no longer viewing?

Chunk-It/Phrased Reading

Fluency: Phrasing

Purpose: To read content phrases seamlessly and cohesively with appropriate pausing

Multiple Intelligences: Visual/spatial, verbal/linguistic, bodily/kinesthetic, interpersonal

Materials: Phrase strips or printed text phrases, highlighter, pen or pencil

Procedure:

1. On phrase strips or printed text phrases, provide printed "chunks"—paragraphs or excerpts of content area, multigenre text (e.g., passages from ethnic authors, variations of problem-solving passages, or varied content texts; see Figure 4.1 for a sample format for presenting the content passages).

2. Ask students to read each phrase independently, keeping in mind they may need to read each cohesive chunk several times before it can be read seamlessly. Encourage students to work in pairs to listen to the oral reading of each content phrase.

Suggested Teacher Talk: *Does the text make sense if I pause after each word? Why or why not? How does pausing at appropriate times enhance understanding?*

3. Encourage students to self-select cohesive chunks of content text to create additional phrase strips. Have students share their phrases with the group.

FIGURE 4.1. Sample Chunk-It Format

The independent and self-assured reader demonstrates fluency, which can correlate with work completion.

The independent and self-assured reader demonstrates fluency, which can correlate with work completion.

The independent and self-assured reader demonstrates fluency, which can correlate with work completion.

The independent and self-assured reader demonstrates fluency, which can correlate with work completion.

The independent and self-assured reader demonstrates fluency, which can correlate with work completion.

Motivation/Engagement: *Musical/rhythmic.* Play appropriate musical excerpts, such as rap or other lyrical selections, that have words from a song or poem, and have students indicate when they hear the end of a phrase.

Slow to Flow

Fluency: Phrasing

Purpose: To use cueing systems to read with appropriate phrasing and expression

Multiple Intelligences: Visual/spatial, verbal/linguistic, interpersonal

Materials: Slow to Flow Guide reproducible (see Appendix), sample content area text excerpts, poetry, charts, and student notebooks or three-ring binder

Procedure:

1. Provide students or student pairs with copies of the Slow to Flow Guide. Students need to maintain their content-specific selections in notebooks or in a three-ring binder.

2. Student pairs take turns reading the initial phrase and reading aloud line by line until completing the entire sentence. As the first student in the pair reads, the second student sits besides that student and reads along independently.

3. Each student silently rereads the last line of the sentence.

4. Students reverse roles and continue until all the sentences have been read.

Suggested Teacher Talk: *Try to capture several words at a time with your eyes ahead of your voice. Read a passage and think about the value of forward eye movement when reading.*

Eye-Voice Span

Fluency: Phrasing

Eye-Voice Span in the Classroom:

Marybeth Witham, an honors chemistry and physical science teacher at a prominent high school, was amazed to see the engagement of her students when they applied the Eye-Voice Span technique with their science content text. She said that because the state performance assessments have a timing element, students not only need the content understanding but also need to have a continuous flow with their reading. Eye-Voice Span has empowered Marybeth to support her students with the ability to phrase the content text more effectively while gathering meaning from the text. The students realized the importance of being conscious of capturing words with their eyes ahead of their voices to monitor their reading process.

Purpose: To recognize and demonstrate the value of forward eye movements when reading

Multiple Intelligences: Visual/spatial, verbal/linguistic, logical/mathematical, body/kinesthetic, interpersonal

Materials: Texts, visual projection device, passage of text; Optional: Phrase Talk Strips reproducible (see Appendix)

Procedure:

1. Discuss with the class the value of peripheral vision when reading. Describe the differences among natural vision (i.e., the way our eyes naturally take in both what is directly in front of us and what is around us in our peripheral vision), peripheral vision, and tunnel vision using a piece of text from your content area. Hold up a piece of text and illustrate natural vision by pointing out that you are using your natural vision to see the page as a whole. Identify peripheral vision by reading aloud and sharing in a think-aloud what is going on with your eyes.

Suggested Teacher Talk: *Think about what your eyes are doing when you are reading. As I am reading aloud with my voice, my eyes are looking ahead—"prereading" the next few words before I say them aloud.*

2. Use a straw to demonstrate tunnel vision by looking through the straw at one word or several letters at a time. Discuss the frustration of trying to gain meaning by looking at only one word at a time.

3. Using a visual projection device, display a text passage from your content area so that all students can see it, and initiate the Eye-Voice Span technique, as described in the following steps (Blevins, 2001; Ellery, 2009). Ask the students to glance at the entire text with their natural vision. All together, begin reading aloud the text.

4. Just before you finish reading a sentence or paragraph, turn off the projector or remove the text from the projector.

Suggested Teacher Talk: *What words are in you holding in your mind, but are no longer presented for you to view?*

5. Have students demonstrate how they can still say the next few words from the passage right after the text is removed. Discuss why this happens (e.g., because students' eyes were ahead of their voices because they were using their peripheral vision).

Suggested Teacher Talk: *Try to "push" your eyes forward, ahead of your voice.*

Motivation/Engagement: *Intrapersonal.* Have students work in A/B pairs (Partner A takes the role of teacher, and Partner B takes the role of student). Partner A listens to Partner B read from the text. Using the Phrase Talk Strips, Partner A randomly places a strip over Partner B's text and then flips the strip to model phrasing talk. Partner B responds to the talk presented on the strip. Have partners take turns sharing what was happening with their eyes as they were reading, what they noticed, or their reactions to the process.

Pausing Punctuation

Purpose: To use punctuation in sentences to support appropriate pausing and enhance meaning

Multiple Intelligences: Visual/spatial, verbal/linguistic, interpersonal

Materials: Content area texts (optional text from www.readwritethink.org); sentences on chart paper, visual projection device, or sentence strips

Procedure:

1. Demonstrate through oral reading how punctuation may cause pausing in different parts of the text, which in turn can alter the meaning of the text. Introduce Pausing Punctuation (Ellery, 2009; Petit, 2003; Strickland, Ganske, & Monroe, 2002): Read the following sentence and discuss how pausing and adding commas could change the meaning of the sentence: *The boy said the man was mad/The boy, said the man, was mad.*

2. Select several sentences from a passage from your content area material and omit the punctuation, or use the text from Martin Luther King Jr.'s "Letter From Birmingham Jail," found in the ReadWriteThink.org lesson entitled "Every Punctuation Mark Matters: A Minilesson on Semicolons."

3. Ask a volunteer to read aloud the selected sentences without pausing.

Suggested Teacher Talk: *Listen to someone read these sentences that are unpunctuated. Try to determine the meaning based on what you heard.*

4. Have students work with partners to revisit the text read, pausing and marking where the proper punctuation should go to make the text clearer and easier to read.

5. Ask pairs to share with the class where they think the punctuation should go based on their interpretation of the correct meaning of the text. Have students return to the text and compare their versions to the original text's punctuation.

Suggested Teacher Talk: *Did your punctuation choices alter the meaning of the original text?*

6. Have students practice reading the original text, paying attention to punctuation and reading accordingly.

Suggested Teacher Talk: *Describe how attending to the punctuation supports you to bring meaning to what is being read.*

Motivation/Engagement: *Logical/mathematical.* Create an organizational chart, such as a three-column chart, to demonstrate the use of punctuation. Ask the students to search content text for examples of the use of the highlighted punctuation. In one column, have them record the highlighted punctuation. In the second column, have them record the example of the punctuation being used in text. In the third column, have the students create their own sentence using the highlighted punctuation.

Fluency Strategy: Scaffolding and Rereading

Scaffolding and Rereading allow the reader to view, hear, and practice fluent reading to gain *confidence* as an independent reader. This support scaffolds the learning while building fluency with *guidance*. The *Reading at Risk* report on adolescent literacy states,

> There are specific methods to improve students' automaticity so that readers can process text with minimal errors. Repeated readings, word accuracy, reading rates, and providing models through paired reading or reading aloud can improve decoding, reading rates, expressive reading, and comprehension of passages that the reader has not seen. (National Association of State Boards of Education, 2006, p. 21)

Applying the scaffolding strategy allows the person modeling reading to demonstrate proper fluency while giving the reader guidance, and more opportunities to practice fluent reading is crucial to the development of a reader. Some adolescent readers need to be motivated intrinsically through *social reading*.

As students repeat their readings, their ability to express improves, and word recognition and reading rate increase (O'Connor, White, & Swanson, 2007; Vadasy & Sanders, 2008). "Musicians, athletes, and actors also use this practice strategy to gain fluency; they *rehearse* the same aspect of their performance repeatedly until they gain independence and confidence" (Ellery, 2009, p. 107, emphasis added). Sharing and collaborating through scaffolding and rereading builds readers' confidence to become fluent readers.

Key Vocabulary for Scaffolding and Rereading

- Confidence: self-assurance in the ability to read text fluently
- Guidance: direction toward becoming fluent
- Rehearse: to prepare and gain confidence through repetition for a fluent reading performance
- Social Reading: engaging in conversations about the text being read

Assessment for Scaffolding and Rereading

Use the following behaviors as a guide as you assess students' abilities to scaffold and reread. Do students exhibit these behaviors never, rarely, often, or always?

☐ Engages in reflective conversations about reading and receives feedback

☐ Imitates modeled reading and self-assesses to evaluate reading

☐ Analyzes repetitive features

Teacher Talk: Statements, Questions, and Prompts for Scaffolding and Rereading

The following are suggestions for teacher talk that encourages readers to think strategically as they employ the scaffolding and rereading strategies. Try using some of these statements, questions, and prompts with your students as you work through the techniques in the following section. They are aligned with Bloom's taxonomy and Webb's DOK levels.

Level of Thinking	Teacher Talk
Creating Extended Thinking	• When you get to an area in the text that does not make sense to you, propose a way to help you comprehend. • Why do readers sometimes need to reread?
Evaluating Strategic Thinking	• Determine the pattern of the text. How does knowing the text structure support your reading?
Analyzing Strategic Thinking	• Compare your first reading with your second or third reading. What do you notice about each time you read the text again?
Applying Skill/Concept	• Listen to the modeled reading. Demonstrate how using the same expression and pace to carry on the story or section supports your understanding of the text.
Understanding Skill/Concept	• What are you thinking about each time you reread a passage? How does hearing the passage first help you?
Remembering Recall	• What is modeled reading?

Techniques for Scaffolding and Rereading

Frontloading

Fluency:
Scaffolding
and Rereading

Purpose: To provide preexposure of the text to increase confidence in the seamless reading of content text

Multiple Intelligences: Visual/spatial, verbal/linguistic, interpersonal, intrapersonal

Materials: Content-specific text at students' instructional reading level

Procedure:

1. Select short, meaningful, appropriate-level text passages aligned with the current content theme or topics. Model the process for annotating the passage(s) with slash marks or sticky notes to align with proper phrasing for fluent reading.

2. Encourage students to preview the passage silently, reflecting on vocabulary, sentence length, and punctuation. Allow appropriate time for students to rehearse the passage and self-reflect on evidence of reading fluency.

Motivation/Engagement: *Logical/mathematical.* Model reading the passage aloud as the students follow in the reading. Remind the students to focus on active listening, proper expressions, and pacing. Using self-reflection, students record their reactions to the reading and share their responses.

Suggested Teacher Talk: *Listen to the modeled reading of each passage. How might you use the same expression and pace as you read further in the story, section, or chapter? What do you notice as you listen to the passage read aloud or preview the text?*

Partner Reading

Purpose: To give and receive support for and feedback on oral reading

Multiple Intelligences: Visual/spatial, verbal/linguistic, interpersonal

Materials: Partner Reading Bookmark (see Appendix), texts

Procedure:

1. To begin Partner Reading (Ellery, 2005; Topping, 2001), pair students as reading partners. An option is to pair students so that one is a stronger reader than the other to match higher and lower need students.

2. Use fluency scores to select partners for reading. Another way to align students' reading levels is to use the five-count rule to determine text difficulty. The student who is not reading holds up five fingers and begins to keep track of the number of errors made in a short passage read by his or her partner. Error correction rule: When the reader is unsure of a word, the partner waits four seconds and then says the word correctly, and the reader repeats the word. This is counted as an error. If partners are unable to identify the word, the word is skipped and still counted as an error.

   Five-Count Guide

   - 0–1 count demonstrates that the book is easy to read

   - 2–3 counts represents that the book is at the reader's interest level

   - 3–4 counts denotes that the book is at the challenge level for understanding

   - 5 count signifies frustration level and the reader should not continue reading until further assistance is given

3. Ask partners to take turns reading aloud to each other, or they may read together while supporting each other's reading throughout the duration of the text being read.

4. Give each student a Partner Reading Bookmark, which lists the reading behaviors. Ask the more fluent reader to use the bookmark as a checklist as his or her partner reads.

Suggested Teacher Talk: *Tell your partner something you notice about yourself when you read.*

5. Partners engage in taking turns reading, rereading, and retelling the assigned passage.

Integrated Choral Reading

Purpose: To view, hear, and rehearse seamless reading of content text to gain confidence as an independent reader

Multiple Intelligences: Visual/spatial, verbal/linguistic, musical/rhythmic, interpersonal

Materials: Content-specific reading text selections, song lyrics, poetry, highlighters, notebook or three-ring binder

Procedure:

1. Model Integrated Choral Reading (Ellery, 2009) using sample content text excerpts to read aloud together. Provide appropriate content passages at the students' instructional or independent reading level.

2. Encourage students to rehearse the passages aloud, striving for seamless, fluent reading.

3. Ask a fluent reader to demonstrate confidence while modeling reading an additional passage. Provide support and encouragement as students reread the passages through choral reading.

4. Students can maintain their content passages in a three-ring binder or choral reading notebook. Choral reading entries can also be used as study guides or as text resources for other fluency techniques described in this chapter.

Suggested Teacher Talk: *How does hearing the passage read aloud support you as a reader?*

5. Compare your initial reading with your second or third reading.

Suggested Teacher Talk: *What do you notice as you rehearse the passages? When you encounter an area of text that does not make sense to you, propose a way to help you comprehend.*

Motivation/Engagement: *Logical/mathematical.* Student pairs alternate roles; one student follows along as his or her partner reads the passage aloud. A paired reading format enhances the amount of rehearsal time provided for reading each passage and provides a social reading format for engaging in discussion of the text. Data can be maintained and added to notebooks in the form of charts or graphs to monitor reading rates on content passages. Note: More on reading rates can be found in the Pacing Strategy section in this chapter.

Fluency Strategy: Expressing

Expressing is another major component of prosody, along with phrasing. Adolescent readers are very expressive in their oral language and understand that the tone in which they make a statement can affect the meaning. When readers begin to use expression as a natural fluency strategy they find the same concept to be true for their reading. The *prosodic functions* (e.g., *pitch, stress, tone*) and forms are valuable for the reader to bring meaning, life, and *purpose* to what is being read. When students apply the expressing strategy to their reading, they are able to convey the text's intended mood and proper meaning. Lack of this strategy leaves the reader sounding monotone and the reading sounding labored. An absence of the expressing strategy also causes many readers to lose their interest and motivation and makes reading feel like a task that is incomprehensible. "Many times concepts appear in ambiguous, confusing language that students can read but do not understand" (Kinniburgh & Shaw, 2007, p. 16). The expressing strategy can encourage adolescent readers to consider learning to read fluently as a meaning-making process. According to Rasinski and Padak (2005), "When students are asked to perform for others, they have a natural inclination and desire to practice the passage to the point where they can read it accurately, with appropriate rate, and especially with meaningful expression and phrasing" (p. 26). The ultimate product is a fluent reader who comprehends what he or she reads and enjoys reading as they become lifelong fluent readers.

Key Vocabulary for Expressing

- Pitch: the tonal height of sound in speech
- Prosodic Function: indication of syntax and attitude from appropriate use of stress, pitch, and tone when reading
- Purpose: the reason or intent for a specific prosodic function being used
- Stress: pronunciation or placement of the accent on spoken words
- Tone: a particular quality of sound created through pitch, modulation, and intonation of the voice

Assessment for Expressing

Use the following behaviors as a guide as you assess students' abilities to express. Do students exhibit these behaviors never, rarely, often, or always?

☐ Identifies prosodic functions

☐ Demonstrates how text comes to life with voice and body language

☐ Conveys the text's mood and meaning

Teacher Talk: Statements, Questions, and Prompts for Expressing

The following are suggestions for teacher talk that encourages readers to think strategically as they employ the expressing strategy. Try using some of these statements, questions, and prompts with your students as you work through the techniques in the following section. They are aligned with Bloom's taxonomy and Webb's DOK levels.

Level of Thinking	Teacher Talk
Creating Extended Thinking	• What message can the volume of your voice send to the audience? How can you modify your voice to sound like you are holding a conversation?
Evaluating Strategic Thinking	• What feeling do you think the author wanted the character to have in this part? How do you know what the author wanted?
Analyzing Strategic Thinking	• Did you use the proper tone to convey the meaning? Why or why not? • How did the tone of your voice set the mood for your statement?
Applying Skill/Concept	• How would the character say that line? • Change your voice to sound like the character you are portraying. • Try to make your reading sound as real as it can be.
Understanding Skill/Concept	• Explain how you can make your reading sound more exciting.
Remembering Recall	• What does a period (or other punctuation mark) mean? • What does your voice do when you read a sentence that ends with a question mark?

Techniques for Expressing

Interpretative Dialogue

Purpose: To apply expressions to portray character traits in text

Multiple Intelligences: Visual/spatial, verbal/linguistic, interpersonal

Materials: Content area text excerpts rich in historical, humorous, fictional, or real-world dialogue

Procedure:

1. Model reading sample dialogue so students have opportunities to hear how to read with expression and how to modify tone and expression for different characters and character

traits. (You might choose sample dialogue from famous speeches, literary works, narratives, and drama.)

2. Ask students to read and rehearse a section of dialogue from content-specific text and craft their own interpretations of how to portray the characters' traits and voices. Encourage students to discuss in small groups their interpretations of the characters and reach a consensus of the analysis of each character. This ensures that meaning is not misconstrued.

3. In groups with established group member character roles, have each student perform the dialogue through the lens of each character, reading aloud with expression.

Suggested Teacher Talk: *Did you use the proper tone to convey the meaning? Why or why not? How can you modify your voice to sound like you are holding a conversation?*

4. After the read-alouds, students are encouraged to read the dialogue selections to each other.

Motivation/Engagement: *Intrapersonal.* Encourage students to self-select additional content area texts that are rich in dialogue and relevant to the current theme or topic of study. After each reading performance, invite the listening audience to reflect on the relationship between the appropriate tone and expression in the dialogue and making meaning of the text.

Suggested Teacher Talk: *What feeling do you think the author wanted the character to present? How might we interpret the intended meaning and attitude in text?*

Totally Tonality

Fluency: Expressing

Purpose: To reflect on and adjust the appropriate tone of voice needed to communicate the intended meaning and attitude in the text.

Multiple Intelligences: Visual/spatial, verbal/linguistic, bodily/kinesthetic

Materials: Expression Cards (see Appendix), content-specific text at students' instructional reading level, note cards, chart paper, visual projection device

Procedure:

1. Ask students to brainstorm words or phrases that describe varied tones that readers use to communicate the author's intended purpose, attitude, or emotion in the text (e.g., sarcastic, humorous, ironic, demonstrative, serious). Point out how the tone of voice reflects the attitude and emotion communicated in the reading using this Totally Tonality technique (Ellery, 2009). Capture key ideas on chart paper, note cards, or the whiteboard to revisit and modify during and after reading.

2. Discuss how the reader's tone of voice can change the communicated meaning of the text. For example, when a phrase such as *very funny* is communicated in a sarcastic tone of voice, it's understood that the speaker is actually saying something is *not* funny.

3. On note cards, write some content-specific phrases that the students can read and write different tones of voice they might use. The teacher may want to include some of the words or phases from the earlier brainstorming activity.

Suggested Teacher Talk: *Modify your voice to sound like the character you are portraying. How did the tone of your voice establish the attitude for your statement?*

4. Encourage students to read appropriate content-specific text selections using a chosen tone. Guide students in noting how the pitch and stress in their voice is used to convey the intended attitude.

5. Discuss the reasons students selected a certain tone when reading each passage.

Suggested Teacher Talk: *What message can the volume of your voice communicate to the audience? What attitude do you feel the author intended to communicate in each passage? How might you know the attitude the author intended?*

Motivation/Engagement: *Interpersonal.* Use the Expression Cards at a writing area. Have the students select several Expression Cards to incorporate into their creative writing. They can write the dialogue of the characters to align with the expressions chosen to convey the proper meaning.

Radio Reading

Purpose: To express dialogue in text through performance-based learning

Multiple Intelligences: Visual/spatial, verbal/linguistic, interpersonal

Materials: Scripted texts; Optional: microphone, radio announcement recordings

Procedure:

1. Assign a content area passage to a group of students to practice reading prior to performing it as a radio announcer for Radio Reading (Ellery, 2009; Greene, 1979; Opitz & Rasinski, 2008; Searfoss, 1975). Only the teacher and the readers have a copy of the scripted text. Those that are participating as the audience (the other students in the class) for the radio show will not have the script to preview. The readers can rehearse at school, home, or both. It may be helpful to have students listen to expressive radio announcements as models for Radio Reading.

2. Have the student radio announcer prepare open-ended questions and statements about the selection. This will allow for dialogue with the audience after the performance.

3. When the radio show is ready to air, hold up a red sign to signal the beginning of the show. The student radio announcer reads the selection (using a microphone if one is available) expressively and meaningfully to capture the listening audience. It is the radio announcer's responsibility to render a clear, comprehensible message.

Suggested Teacher Talk: *How can you make your reading sound more exciting?*

4. Invite the audience into a discussion about the selection using the questions and statements the student radio announcer provides. Discussing the questions and statements requires the listening audience to demonstrate if they derived meaning from the reading.

Suggested Teacher Talk: *What message can the volume of your voice send to the audience?*

Readers Theatre

Purpose: To explore expressive language use through oral reading of scripts

Multiple Intelligences: Visual/spatial, verbal/linguistic, interpersonal

Materials: Texts, scripts; Optional: microphones

Procedure:

1. Provide students with a dialogue-rich script of a story derived from text that may be prepared for Readers Theatre (Hoyt, 1992; Shepard, 1994; Sloyer, 1982). You might select text right from a story, have students generate a script based on content text, or provide a script you created. There are numerous websites available from which you can download scripts. The students need to have a clear understanding of the types of adjustments (e.g., use of quotations, dialogue, Readers Theatre script) that were made to change the text into a play.

2. Assign the students roles in the play. Highlight the text for each reader's role on a separate copy of the script. Give students the option to read the original text and then the newly scripted version to help them compare and contrast the dramatization that they will need to perform the Readers Theatre. These selections should contain interesting characters, appealing themes, and stimulating plots that enhance language.

3. Discuss with students the meaning of the text and the importance of the use of language.

Suggested Teacher Talk: *How would the character say that line? Change your voice to sound like the character you are portraying. Try to make your reading sound as real as it can be.*

4. Allow students many opportunities to rehearse their parts before "going public" by reading aloud. Encourage reading with expression. Remind them that they do not have to memorize their parts prior to the performance. They will be holding the script and reading directly from the text. It is each student's responsibility to bring the character to life with prosodic features.

5. After several rehearsals, have students, individually or in small groups, perform a dramatized presentation, *expressively* reading their parts in front of a live audience. Following the performance, give feedback on how the students portrayed the characters with their expressions.

Suggested Teacher Talk: *Did you use the proper tone to convey the meaning? Why or why not? How did the tone of your voice set the mood for your statement?*

Motivation/Engagement: *Logical/mathematical.* Invite students to adapt a piece of literature into a script for Readers Theatre. Have them create guidelines or criteria for reading expressively, which the group can use while preparing for their Readers Theatre. Criteria might include the following: work cooperatively as group prepares and rehearses, speak clearly and use an appropriate volume, read the text accurately and with proper expressions.

Fluency Strategy: Pacing

Appropriate pacing is vital to a fluent reader's ability to bring meaning to the text. Pacing includes the reader's *rate, flexibility* with the text to *alter* the pace as needed to comprehend, and the reader's *automaticity* while encountering words. "Show me a thoughtful reader who adjusts his pace according to prior knowledge and text structure, and I'll show you a real reader" (Marcell, 2010, p. 1). When readers slow down to attend to unfamiliar words, they lose meaning of what has already been read, and their comprehension decreases (O'Connor et al., 2007; Rasinski, 2000; Vadasy & Sanders, 2008). Recent practices have encouraged readers to "*speed*" read text to increase their words-correct-per-minute rate. However, in order for proper pacing to enhance proficient reading, it is important to avoid reading too fast (being a word caller) and instead to read at a pace that *flows* as meaning is formulated. Text that is at the student's independent or instructional level is needed when applying the pacing strategy.

Key Vocabulary for Pacing

- Alter: to adjust pacing to bring meaning to the text
- Automaticity: instant word recognition with accuracy and flow
- Flexibility: ability to adapt rate to determine meaning
- Flow: to move consistently, smoothly, and freely from word to word
- Rate: speed, tempo, or time in which words are read automatically
- Speed: number of words read correctly per minute (WCPM)

Assessment for Pacing

Use the following behaviors as a guide as you assess students' abilities to pace. Do students exhibit these behaviors never, rarely, often, or always?

- ☐ Distinguishes appropriate rhythm in reading
- ☐ Adjusts reading rate
- ☐ Tracks and observes the flow of reading

Teacher Talk: Statements, Questions, and Prompts for Pacing

The following are suggestions for teacher talk that encourages readers to think strategically as they employ the pacing strategy. Try using some of these statements, questions, and prompts with your students as you work through the techniques in the following section. They are aligned with Bloom's taxonomy and Webb's DOK levels.

Level of Thinking	Teacher Talk
Creating Extended Thinking	• How does the speed at which you are reading make a difference for you? • Formulate a plan to adapt your pacing as you read.
Evaluating Strategic Thinking	• What criteria do you use to determine if you are pacing appropriately? • How effective is your rate of reading?
Analyzing Strategic Thinking	• Listen to these sentences being read aloud and track the pace of the reading in your copy of the text. Is it easy or difficult for you to keep up with the pace being modeled—that is, with the tempo?
Applying Skill/Concept	• Try to follow the light I'm shining on the text as I read and maintain the same pace to increase your rate.
Understanding Skill/Concept	• Explain how hearing yourself read and tracking how long it takes you to read helps you to pace better. • How does increasing your rate help you?
Remembering Recall	• What is your reading rate?

 ## Techniques for Pacing

Rate/Record/Reflect

Fluency: Pacing

Purpose: To self-monitor flow of reading

Multiple Intelligences: Visual/spatial, verbal/linguistic

Materials: Methods for Determining Developmental Reading Levels (see Appendix), texts, photocopies of text, stopwatch, audio recorder (e.g., iPhone, voice recorder), graph paper

Procedure:

1. *Rate:* Have each student read aloud a text at his or her developmental reading level while you or a volunteer time the student with a stopwatch. On graph paper, chart the time it took the student to read the text (Allington, 2001; Ellery, 2009). Use Table 4.1 to determine

TABLE 4.1. Reading Performance Levels and Accuracy Rate

Reading Performance Levels	Accuracy Rate
Independent	95–100% (able to read without assistance)
Instructional	90–94% (able to read with some assistance)
Frustration	89% and below (unable to read even with assistance)

Note. Word accuracy rate = number of words read – number of errors ÷ number of words read.

TABLE 4.2. Oral Reading Fluency Rate, Grades 5–12, Words Correct Per Minute (WCPM)

Grade	Percentile	Fall WCPM	Winter WCPM	Spring WCPM
5	90	169	184	194
	50	117	131	137
	10	61	74	83
6	90	177	195	204
	50	127	140	150
	10	68	82	93
7	90	180	192	202
	50	128	136	150
	10	79	88	98
8	90	185	199	204
	50	133	146	151
	10	77	84	97
9[a]	(silent)	180	190	214
10	(silent)	190	214	224
11	(silent)	214	224	237
12	(silent)	224	237	250

Note. Words correct per minute = number of words in the passage ÷ reading time (in seconds) × 60.
Adapted from an electronic aggregation using AIMSweb Norms 2003–2009; Hasbrouck & Tindal, 2006; Johns & Berglund, 2006.
[a]The oral reading rates are listed only to eighth grade. Typically, oral reading rate does not increase beyond eighth grade. Therefore, the rates listed for grades 9–12 are for silent reading and percentiles are not included.

the student's accuracy rate and Table 4.2 to find the reading rate that correlates with a grade level.

Suggested Teacher Talk: *Explain how increasing your rate will help your reading.*

2. *Record*: Have each student record the same reading on an audio recorder and time his or her reading. The student should play the recording while following along using a photocopied version of the text. Have the student note miscues, which represent a

departure from the text, on the photocopy and score their errors. Reflecting on miscue analysis allows the reader to examine the type of miscues (e.g., omissions, mispronunciations, repetition). Reading errors are specific miscues that are scored that alter the meaning of the text (e.g. insertions, substitutions). Chart the time for the second reading on graph paper.

Suggested Teacher Talk: *How does hearing yourself read and tracking how long it takes you to read help you to pace better?*

3. *Reflect*: Ask the students to compare their reading times and continue the previous steps as needed. Share with students that they should expect an increase in their reading rate as they are rereading the passage.

Motivation/Engagement: *Intrapersonal.* Have students reflect on and self-assess the reading and the graphed results. Repeat the process two more times. Have students create goals for themselves as they note their progress. Additional fluency assessments can be used to determine not only their reading rate but also reading level. The following are a few examples of fluency assessments for secondary readers:

- *Qualitative Reading Inventory-4* (Leslie & Caldwell, 2005)
- *3-Minute Reading Assessments: Word Recognition, Fluency, and Comprehension, Grades 5–8* (Rasinski & Padak, 2005)
- *Developmental Reading Assessment, 4–8*, second edition (Beaver & Carter, 2003)

Beam Reading

Purpose: To use an instrument to visually guide reading and gauge flow

Multiple Intelligences: Visual/spatial, verbal/linguistic, interpersonal

Materials: Texts, laser-beam pen or flashlight

Procedure:

1. Use a laser-beam pen or flashlight to shine on words in a selected text. Move the light along the words at a steady pace. Students can also have their own flashlight for individual reading.

Suggested Teacher Talk: *Try to keep up with the light to increase your rate.*

2. Encourage students to follow along with the light as they read aloud. Increase the rate at which the light shines on the words with each rereading of the text.

3. Have students practice this technique with partners, taking turns beaming light on the sentences and reading silently or aloud at the pace of the light.

Suggested Teacher Talk: *Is it easy or hard for you to keep up with the pace being modeled? How does the speed at which you are reading make a difference for you? Formulate a plan to adapt your pacing as you read.*

Sprints and Stamina

Sprints and Stamina in the Classroom:

Mandy Kersey, a high school reading teacher, uses Sprints and Stamina as a technique with every ability range, from the struggling special needs student or ESOL student who is practicing basic reading skills to the gifted student who is getting prepared for Advanced Placement exams or college entrance exams. Mandy shares with her students the terms *sprints* and *stamina* as used by runners: Sprints help them run faster and increase stamina, or endurance, in their track training. She explains that students are going to use a similar technique in their classroom for fluency training. She lets her students know that just as runners must use specific practices to increase their ability levels, good readers must also train their brains with effective reading strategies.

Purpose: To be flexible with reading rate to enhance meaning and endurance

Multiple Intelligences: Visual/spatial, verbal/linguistic, interpersonal, intrapersonal

Materials: Clipboard, whistle, content area leveled text, paper; Optional: stopwatch or timer

Procedure:

1. Distribute text to each student for reading. Explain to the students that the sprint concept relates to running a short distance at a fast pace. The goal of sprints is to get the students to practice reading as quickly as they can in a short time period. The range of time can be one-, two-, or three-minute increments. The reading is timed. Students will read as quickly as they can, then record their word correct per minute (WCPM) rate. The goal is to increase speed while maintaining a certain level of accuracy in comprehension. (The accuracy level can be moved based on specific ability, but should be at least 70%.)

2. Demonstrate the sprint concept applied to reading by asking the students to use several strategies that support pacing their reading without sacrificing meaning of content.

   Variations of sprints:

   - *Relay Sprints*: Students are in a group of four. They read a short passage, and when one minute is up, they must pass the paper to the next person. At the end of four minutes, they discuss the four passages as a group and work together to answer a list of questions about the passage without looking at the passage.

   - *Interval Sprints*: Students read for one minute, then for two minutes, then for three, then for four (and the time *can* go back down). At the end of each interval they have a brief rest to answer the questions. They then compare their WCPM and accuracy at each level.

   - *Who/What/When/Where/Why Sprints*: Students read the passage as before, but instead of having predesigned questions, the students must simply answer Who/What/When/Where/Why about the passage to show they comprehend the meaning.

- *Vocabulary/Review Sprints*: Create a template with the vocabulary, terms, or characters that the students need to study or remember. Make several different versions of the template, with the terms in a different order on each version. Time the students for one minute as they read as many of the terms as they can before time is called. After time is called, students rotate papers so that they have a new sheet with the terms in a different order. Repeat two to three times to help study and increase reading speed.

- *Oral Sprints*: Students read a passage aloud in one minute to see how many words they can read verbally. The teacher circles on his or her own paper any mistakes that are made during the reading and documents how the student read. Questions of comprehension immediately are given verbally.

3. Explain to the students the concept of stamina by relating it to running a long-distance race. The goal of stamina is to help students endure longer reading passages and be able to recall information from longer texts, while still reading at a certain pace. Passages for stamina need to be at least 500 to 750 words and can be up to 2,500 words. The number of words is directly tied to how strong a reader the student is, and it should increase over time.

4. Model several stamina ideas applied to reading by asking the students to use several strategies that support pacing reading without sacrificing meaning of content.

   Variations of stamina:

   - *ACT Preparation*: Choose passages that are 750 words and create 10 questions about them. The passages must include one relating to prose fiction, one to social science, one to the humanities, and one to natural science. Students will need to be able to complete each passage and respond to the 10 questions in less than 8½ minutes, because that is how long they will have on the actual ACT test.

   - *Novel Stamina*: This can be done in class or at home. Students time themselves reading a chapter in a novel that is at an appropriate reading level. They can count four lines and then create an average based on the total number of lines. This may help them get through a book that they are having a hard time reading.

   - *Low-Level Stamina*: These are shorter passages at a reading level one grade level below the student's actual ability. This is done to increase confidence in reading and to help them increase flow.

   - *Prepared Stamina*: Students preview the passage and have the opportunity to skim the passage and look for any unfamiliar or unknown words before reading. Students may use several resources to help them (e.g., dictionary, translation dictionary) before beginning the passage. Students are given a predetermined amount of preparation time as needed. They will then be timed and tested as usual.

Commercial Programs

Purpose: To practice smooth reading using technology and other resources

Multiple Intelligences: Visual/spatial, verbal/linguistic, bodily/kinesthetic

Materials: Texts, computer, computer-based program

Procedure:

1. Select an appropriate computer program (see the following list). The programs listed are supplemental and may be used for immediate, intense intervention in several of the areas of reading noted in Chapters 3–6.

2. Incorporate one of the following computer-based fluency programs into your comprehensive literacy-based classroom.

Suggested Teacher Talk: *Does the computer program help you pace yourself as a reader? Why or why not? How does the speed to which you are reading make a difference for you?*

- *Great Leaps Reading Program* (K–12; Campbell & Mercer, 1998) is a tutorial program divided into three major areas: (1) phonics, which concentrates on developing and mastering essential sight–sound relationships or sound-awareness skills, (2) sight phrasing, which supports students in mastering sight words while developing and improving focusing skills, and (3) reading fluency, which provides age-appropriate stories specifically designed to build reading fluency, reading motivation, and proper intonation.

- *Inside: Language, Literacy, and Content* (4–8; National Geographic School Publishing, 2008) provides daily practice in routines for developing reading accuracy, intonation, phrasing, expression, and rate.

- *QuickReads* (Hiebert, 2005) is composed of high-interest nonfiction texts at the second- through sixth-grade levels. QuickReads develops automaticity by using text that is composed of 98% high-frequency and decodable words. The program combines leveled texts with speech-recognition technology. The program provides instant feedback and corrects errors by prompting repeated pronunciation of unknown words.

- *REWARDS* (Reading Excellence Word Attack and Rate Development Strategies; Archer, Gleason, & Vachon, 2000) is intended for intermediate to secondary students. It supports students in decoding and reading multisyllabic words in context, increasing reading accuracy and fluency, and improving comprehension. The first 12 lessons support the skills necessary to learn multisyllabic words (blending syllables and pronunciations of affixes and vowel combinations). The last 7 lessons focus on helping readers use fast and accurate decoding to increase reading rate.

Fluency Strategy: Wide Reading

Students need an opportunity to read a *variety of genres* and structures as they *discover* the joy of wide reading to contribute to improved fluency. Wide reading stems from a need for a variety of literary genres to increase *motivation*, fluency, and comprehension. The more exposure readers have to text, the more opportunities will arise for them to *engage* with a text that motivates them to read. The practices of providing students with access to appropriate texts as well as opportunities to read texts that are engaging and age appropriate are essential for effective fluency instruction (Tatum, 2008). Wide reading exposes the readers to a plethora of words, increasing *word consciousness* and accuracy for fluency development. Content texts often contain specialized terms that may be unfamiliar to readers and therefore slow their reading. Using the strategy of wide reading draws students' attention to new vocabulary as they become aware of the precise word usage. Research by Nathan and Stanovich (1991) indicates that

> [if students are] to become fluent readers, they need to read a lot. Our job as educators is to see to it that children want to read, that they seek new knowledge via the written word and derive satisfaction and joy from the reading process. (p. 179)

Key Vocabulary for Wide Reading

- Discover: to find interest in text

- Engage: to actively attend to text

- Motivation: the desire, passion, and reason to read

- Variety of Genres: different categories of types of text

- Word Consciousness: awareness of words being used

Assessment for Wide Reading

Use the following behaviors as a guide as you assess students' abilities to employ wide reading techniques. Do students exhibit these behaviors never, rarely, often, or always?

☐ Chooses to read independently

☐ Self-selects books based on reading level

☐ Determines purpose for reading

Teacher Talk: Statements, Questions, and Prompts for Wide Reading

The following are suggestions for teacher talk that encourages readers to think strategically as they employ the wide reading strategy. Try using some of these statements, questions, and

prompts with your students as you work through the techniques in the following section. They are aligned with Bloom's taxonomy and Webb's DOK levels.

Level of Thinking	Teacher Talk
Creating Extended Thinking	• Create an organizational chart or guide of traits that you look for when selecting a book. How do you determine if the text is aligned with your reading level?
Evaluating Strategic Thinking	• How do you feel when you are reading a book that is at your level? • Why is it important to independently read books at your appropriate level?
Analyzing Strategic Thinking	• Distinguish the characteristics of a book that is considered a challenge for you, compared with a book that is more in your comfort zone.
Applying Skill/Concept	• Try to select a book that interests you and is in your comfort zone. • Record in your reading logs the variety of genres you are reading.
Understanding Skill/Concept	• What are signs that a book is too easy or too difficult for you?
Remembering Recall	• Identify several genres you are reading.

Techniques for Wide Reading

Volume Reading

Purpose: To be exposed to a variety of reading for extensive independent reading

Multiple Intelligences: Visual/spatial, verbal/linguistic, intrapersonal

Materials: Pass the Book Reflection Guide reproducible (see Appendix), multigenre content area leveled texts (e.g., varied genre formats of relevant trade books, reference materials, Web resources, newspapers, magazines), notebooks or three-ring binders

Procedure:

1. Select relevant, multigenre texts that support and enhance the current content theme or topic of study. Students should have easy, frequent access to these resources to encourage extensive engagement with level-appropriate texts (e.g., comic books, trade books, fiction, nonfiction).

2. Engage students in a "pass-the-book" process to pique their interest and desire to read. Arrange the classroom in a small-group environment and place a sampling of the selected text resources at each group table. Ensure that a diverse sampling of genres is included for each group.

Suggested Teacher Talk: *Try to select text that interests you and is at your comfort zone. Record the variety of genres you are reading.*

3. Model the process for digging into a text resource by determining the genre, reading the book jacket, previewing the first few pages of the text, and determining the match between the text and the reader.

4. Provide each student with a Pass the Book Reflection Guide for listing the titles and authors of books they would want to read. The Pass the Book Reflection Guide can be maintained in a journal or notebook for accountability and self-regulating of the reading volume. Students should be reminded to refer to their journals for new titles and additional reading.

5. Students move from table to table to peruse the book selections, noting on their Pass the Book Reflection Guide titles and authors of books of interest. Depending on class size and room arrangement, an option is for students to work in small groups. In this case, provide six to eight books for each group to explore. After exploring the available books (for approximately 8–10 minutes) groups can pass the books to another group and repeat the process with a different sampling of books.

6. Periodically revisit the pass-the-book process to encourage students to update and increase their volume of reading selections and share both new titles and recently read selections with their group.

Suggested Teacher Talk: *What are indicators or signs that a book is too easy or too difficult for you? Why is important to independently read books at your appropriate level?*

Motivation/Engagement: *Interpersonal.* Market the books by periodically featuring selected content text resources. Model how to highlight books and resources by reading a dramatic text excerpt, sharing illustrations, or doing both. Students can replicate this process of marketing books and titles they found particularly interesting.

Scaffolding

Fluency: Wide Reading

Purpose: To use support when aligning reading level with appropriate text difficulty

Multiple Intelligences: Visual/spatial, verbal/linguistic, interpersonal

Materials: Methods for Determining Developmental Reading Levels (see Appendix), variety of leveled texts (e.g., content book excerpts, journal articles)

Procedure:

1. Select a group of students to work in a small-group setting at or slightly above their independent reading levels. Group students who have similar needs or interests. Use the Methods for Determining Developmental Reading Levels reproducible to determine students' levels for grouping.

2. Choose texts that are accessible on the basis of appropriate grammar, rhetorical structure, vocabulary, and background knowledge of students and texts that are engaging and interesting.

3. Model how to select a book or text that is just the right match for the student's level. Discuss why it is important to evaluate reading material to determine if it is at the appropriate level.

Suggested Teacher Talk: *What are signs that a book is too easy or too difficult for you?*

4. Model the use of a reading strategy with the text (e.g., determining importance) and discuss why the strategy is appropriate for understanding the text.

5. Have students read a selection from the text independently, practicing previously introduced teaching points for the strategy. Return to the text together and analyze the application of the teaching point. Students can reread text for fluency after scaffolding to increase independent wide reading.

Literary Tours

Purpose: To pique interest and motivation for reading a wide variety of content area text resources

Fluency:
Wide Reading

Multiple Intelligences: Visual/spatial, verbal/linguistic, interpersonal, intrapersonal, naturalist/ environmentalist

Materials: Multigenre, appropriate content area text resources (e.g., websites, magazines, newspapers, books) and other resources aligned with the current theme or topic, chart paper, whiteboard, or visual projection device

Procedure:

1. Encourage students to share varied locations (real-world or historical) relevant to the current content area theme or topic that they would like to tour virtually. Capture students' ideas on chart paper, a whiteboard, or a visual projection device.

2. Support students in brainstorming what they might see, hear, and discover on the virtual tour of their chosen destination (e.g., Independence Hall and Liberty Bell Center in Philadelphia, Pennsylvania: A visitor may see the Liberty Bell and crowds of visitors and hear the voice of a curator or tour guide. A visitor may discover the historical significance of the signing of the Declaration of Independence.).

3. Students brainstorm and identify multigenre print and online resources that can be used as references to extend understanding of their destination.

Suggested Teacher Talk: *Identify several multigenre text resources that you might read to extend your understanding as you tour your destination. What essential questions would you want answered during your literary tour?*

4. Select content area text resources relevant to the current theme or topic. Encourage students to seek additional reading resources to extend their exploration.

5. Guide students to transfer the tour concept to one or more of the nonfiction text resources they will be reading. Students tour their location through reading.

Suggested Teacher Talk: *Describe some of the key ideas as you are reading.*

Content Read-Aloud

Fluency:
Wide Reading

Purpose: To absorb key vocabulary through modeling of expressive, enthusiastic reading as well as to experience the pleasure of reading

Multiple Intelligences: Visual/spatial, verbal/linguistic, interpersonal

Materials: Level-appropriate, content-specific text, note cards

Procedure:

1. Select multigenre, content-specific text resources (e.g., newspaper and magazine articles, textbook or literature excerpts, children's books) that you find interesting and read them aloud to students. Encourage students to focus on the vivid expression and tonality as you read and to absorb the content vocabulary from the read-aloud (Ellery, 2009; Kane, 2007).

2. Instruct students to discuss with a partner the interesting words and phrases, tone, and expression heard during the read-aloud.

Suggested Teacher Talk: *How does the expression, tone, and pace of the oral reading support understanding? Why are our featured vocabulary words interesting to you?*

3. Make the text accessible in the classroom for students to revisit and read independently. Maintain a list or chart of content text titles read aloud in class. Focus on providing read-aloud resources from a variety of genres.

Motivation/Engagement: *Intrapersonal.* Provide note cards for students to capture and record interesting vocabulary after the teacher has finished reading. This academic vocabulary can be used as seeds for discussion as well as for activating background knowledge of the topic or theme.

Chapter 5

Vocabulary: Making Meaningful Connections

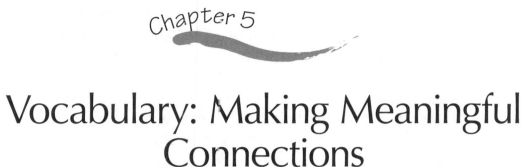

Associating with
Active Analogies

Contextualizing with
Context Complex Clues

Associating with **Academic Word Wall**

The necessity for effective vocabulary instruction becomes increasingly evident in intermediate and secondary classrooms as readers engage with the specialized vocabulary presented in content area text. Secondary readers often struggle with the academic language (Marzano & Pickering, 2005) and require many opportunities for developing rich, expressive (speaking and writing), receptive (listening and reading), and technical (content area related) vocabulary. A report by the National Institute for Literacy (2007) confirms the complexity of understanding content area literacy for adolescent learners. A growing research base evinces the alignment of a rich vocabulary and a student's ability to make connections in reading. The intersection between vocabulary knowledge and comprehension is extended by presenting vocabulary as influencing comprehension and fluency and as a consistent predictor of comprehension (Beck, McKeown, & Kucan, 2008; Blachowicz & Fisher, 2006; Nagy & Scott, 2000; NICHD, 2000; Pearson, Hiebert, & Kamil, 2007). Educators recognize that vocabulary words are at the heart of learning in content classrooms because new terms represent the concepts being taught.

Academic language may present roadblocks for adolescent readers, as "many words that seem familiar to students carry a completely different meaning when encountered in subject areas, a meaning which might be completely unrelated to what students understand in real life, disabling the usefulness of prior knowledge" (Kossack, 2007, p. 199). Integrating vocabulary instruction provides students with numerous opportunities to manipulate and extend usage of content-specific terminology. Infusing vocabulary instruction across disciplines provides multiple encounters for students to make connections to new and already known information, discuss meanings, and demonstrate appropriate applications. It is essential to encourage students to think strategically when learning new words. Vocabulary knowledge is cumulative and requires reexposures in a variety of meaningful contexts to have a profound effect on student comprehension. Educators can structure the process for students to think strategically when learning new words.

This chapter offers vocabulary strategies and techniques that support comprehensive vocabulary instruction to enhance students' understanding of new terminology, academic vocabulary, and concepts. Students can benefit from intentional support to command the vast reading and oral vocabulary required of 21st-century learners. These strategies will provide students with powerful, in-depth learning as they strive to become successful readers. Graves (2009) articulates the importance of vocabulary: "Possessing and using a powerful vocabulary helps us better understand others, be better understood by others, and enjoy the richness of the English language" (p. 3).

To effectively use the vocabulary strategies and techniques presented in this chapter, ample time should be allotted for teacher modeling, student engagement, and scaffolding of learning. The goal is to structure instruction to support independent application and student ownership of learning.

Teachers can use the Motivation/Engagement section within many techniques as an additional means of motivating the whole learner and creating 21st-century secondary learners (refer to Chapter 1 for a description of the whole learner and to Figure 1.1 for an illustration of the composition of a 21st-century secondary learner). The Motivation/ Engagement section allows for differentiation within the technique as needed to meet the needs of all learners. The section identifies and uses a multiple intelligence other than those that are highlighted in the main procedure of the technique.

Educators should use these vocabulary strategies and techniques within the planning and instructional process. However, it is essential to understand that these strategies and techniques are multifaceted and can be interchangeable within the components of lesson planning (before, during, and after instruction). The vocabulary techniques support secondary readers to sustain independence as readers and acquire the reading strategies.

The following are the strategies and techniques in this chapter:

- Associating: Active Analogies, Word-Net Wheel, Semantic Feature Analysis, Fusion, Academic Word Wall

- Contextualizing: Content Multiple Meaning, Inferring Word Meaning, Context Complex Clues, Inquisitive Stance

- Visualizing: Four Corners, Sensory Scenery, Mind's Eye, Mind Maps

- Personalizing: Knowledge Rating, Genre Jive, Word Tech

- Referencing: Start Your Engines, Resource Course, Defining Moment

Vocabulary Strategy: Associating

Word associating allows the reader to form a *word-net framework* to make *connections* and determine *word relationships*. Understanding this network of words expands the reader's ability to analyze and *synthesize* the text information being read: "The students who can associate the words with each other can expand their vocabulary and choose the right word for the right context" (Istifci, 2010, p. 364). When readers use *analogies* and make associations among words, it influences the learning of word meaning. A reader processes in a "*linguistic* form that includes print and meaning and nonlinguistic form that includes visual and sensory images" (Bromley, 2007, p. 531; emphasis added). This strategy supports the reader's ability to increase the semantic value of their word-fabric internal system, creating a tapestry of meaning to every verbal and nonverbal means of communication. It is vital that secondary readers continuously sew words together to bring meaning to the content they are reading.

When making associations among words, readers begin to create categories to organize new concepts and experiences in relation to prior knowledge. Readers are supported by applying a variety of graphic word organizers as visual representations of the identified relationships: "The limits of the learner's cognitive capacity should be addressed in the design of graphic organizers" (Stull & Mayer, 2007, p. 818). Associating allows students to internalize the patterns under study and begin to *categorize*, make connections, and promote cognitive word knowledge (Ellery, 2009; Miller & Eilam, 2008; Strickland et al., 2002).

Key Vocabulary for Associating

- Analogy: a comparison; standardization of linguistic forms

- Categorize: to use higher order thinking to organize words by essential attributes, qualities, and characteristics of the words' meanings

- Connection: a link between words, based on prior knowledge, to broaden word meaning

- Linguistic: related to the study of natural language; incorporates the structure of grammar

- Synthesize: to fuse, create, and produce meaning by combining understanding of words

- Word Relationships: connections among words; can be based on their similarities, differences, or other characteristics

- Word-Net Framework: an interconnected word meaning system

Assessment for Associating

Use the following behaviors as a guide as you assess students' abilities to associate. Do students exhibit these behaviors never, rarely, often, or always?

☐ Determines how words relate and connects ideas to form the meanings of words

☐ Generates analogies to extend content knowledge

☐ Chooses and categorizes words by specific features

Teacher Talk: Statements, Questions, and Prompts for Associating

The following are suggestions for teacher talk that encourages readers to think strategically as they employ the associating strategy. Try using some of these statements, questions, and prompts with your students as you work through the techniques in the following section. They are aligned with Bloom's taxonomy and Webb's DOK levels.

Level of Thinking	Teacher Talk
Creating Extended Thinking	• Construct other examples that demonstrate the same analogy and theorize the structure that connects the words. • Create a graphic word organizer to demonstrate your understanding of the words.
Evaluating Strategic Thinking	• Check with a partner to see if you both agree about associations of these words. • What information would you use to support your view of how these words are related?
Analyzing Strategic Thinking	• Examine the features of the words. What does the similarity tell you about these features and about what these words have in common? • Distinguish what connects all these examples.
Applying Skill/Concept	• Create a word that corresponds with _____. • What other words have the same relationship as the example words?

Understanding	• Think about these words and how they are associated.
Skill/Concept	• This word [say the word] is to this word [say the word]. Describe why these words are connected.
	• What comes to mind when you think of this word?
Remembering Recall	• What are examples and nonexamples of the word (i.e., synonyms and antonyms)?
	• What does it mean to fuse a word?

Techniques for Associating

Active Analogies

Purpose: To recognize the relationship between the words in a word pair

Multiple Intelligences: Visual/spatial, logical/mathematical, bodily/kinesthetic, interpersonal

Materials: Active Analogies reproducible (see Appendix), Reflection Connection Puzzle Piece reproducible (see Appendix), context text, note cards

Procedure:

1. From content-specific text, select words, concepts, or symbols that have similar relationships (see Figure 5.1 for a sample Reflection Connection analogy).

2. Write each analogy's set of words on Reflection Connection Puzzle Pieces (one word on each piece) and cut the puzzle pieces apart.

3. Model the use of one puzzle set by introducing the words, concepts, or symbols and explaining how they relate; model the think-aloud to activate higher order engagement.

Suggested Teacher Talk: *Think about these words and how they are associated. This word [say the word] is to this word [say the word]. What is the relationship between the two words?*

FIGURE 5.1. Sample Reflection Connection Analogy

LANGSTON HUGHES: POETRY :: AARON COPELAND: _____

LIE: PREVARICATE :: DELAY: _____

DENTIST: PHYSICAL :: PSYCHOLOGIST: _____

ARTIST: ROCKWELL :: _____: ROWLING

CLUMSY: GRACEFUL :: AWKWARD: _____

FEEBLE: WEAK :: _____: CONTEMPLATIVE

UNFATHOMABLE: COMPREHENSIBLE :: _____: DISTANT

4. Students think of two additional words that have the same relationship to each other. Write an analogy sentence to begin the connection to demonstrate the connections among the words (i.e., _____ is to _____ as _____ is to _____). For example, in the content area of mathematics, a "purpose" relationship could be "ruler is to line as compass is to circle" (i.e., the purpose of a ruler is to measure a line, and the purpose of a compass is to measure a circle).

5. Have students make analogy predictions based on the earlier discussion of how the two words are related. Show the analogy symbols and their meanings to provide a visual imprint of formal representation of analogies (i.e., : [single colon] means "is to" and :: [double colon] means "as"): _____ : _____ :: _____ : _____ .

6. Divide students into two groups and give each student a puzzle piece. Students in group A get the left-side puzzle piece words (e.g., *ruler*), and students in group B get the right-side puzzle piece words (e.g., *line*), which are related to the words held by students in group A.

7. Students read the word on their puzzle pieces and find their partners from the opposite group—the person who holds the puzzle piece with a related word. Once the partners have been formed, have them create an analogy sentence and record their results on the Active Analogies reproducible. Encourage students to use content-specific words for their sample analogies.

Motivation/Engagement: *Intrapersonal.* Students craft additional content analogies and determine the appropriate categories for each analogy set by creating mental models. They can create "Jeopardy" question cards to be compiled for a class Analogy "Jeopardy" Board (see Figure 5.2). Students can also create an analogy collage to demonstrate pictorial analogies.

FIGURE 5.2. Sample Analogy "Jeopardy" Board

Authors	Lit. Terms	Lit. Works	Issues	Potpourri
100	100	100	100	100
200	200	200	200	200
300	300	300	300	300
400	400	400	400	400
500	500	500	500	500

Word-Net Wheel

Purpose: To compare words and determine their relationships

Multiple Intelligences: Visual/spatial, interpersonal

Materials: Word-Net Wheel reproducible (see Appendix), text

Procedure:

1. Select sets of words that relate to one another and record these words on index cards. Make copies of the Word-Net Wheel and distribute a copy to each student or to each group at a table, along with the word cards.

2. Have the students read their set of words and write each word on one of the spokes of the Word-Net Wheel reproducible. Ask the students to write what they know about each word in the open area between each spoke.

3. Ask the students to reflect on the words on the wheel collectively. Have them determine the relationship, attributes, and characteristics of the words on the wheel and categorize the words with a title.

Suggested Teacher Talk: *Examine the characteristics of the words. What similarities can you find in these features? What do these words have in common? Distinguish what connects all these examples.*

4. Have students share with the whole group their Word-Net Wheels. Lead a discussion about what students wrote on their wheels and how these ideas supported their process of making meaning for the words.

Motivation/Engagement: *Logical/mathematical.* Students can create Concept Circles (Allen, 2007; Vacca, Vacca, & Gove, 2000). Invite students to select four words from the topic of study, divide a circle into four equal sections, and write one of the words in each section. Ask students to describe the meanings and relationships between and among the Concept Circle words to demonstrate content knowledge. They should summarize their descriptions in student journals or notebooks.

Semantic Feature Analysis

Purpose: To explore the relationships among sets of essential vocabulary, elicit prior knowledge, make predictions, and monitor comprehension

Multiple Intelligences: Visual/spatial, verbal/linguistic, logical/mathematical, interpersonal

Materials: Semantic Feature Analysis Matrix reproducible (see Appendix), content text; Optional: student notebooks or journals, visual projection device, computer and online resources such as ReadWriteThink.org lesson titled "Guided Comprehension: Knowing How Words Work Using Semantic Feature Analysis"

Procedure:

1. Select essential phrases or individual words and list them vertically on the left axis of the Semantic Feature Analysis Matrix (Baldwin, Ford, & Readence, 1981; Buehl, 2001; Frey & Fisher, 2004; Pittelman, Heimlich, Berglund, & French, 1991). Consider key concepts that represent larger ideas students will encounter as they read the content text. Gradually move toward more abstract ideas.

2. Provide each student with a copy of the Semantic Feature Analysis Matrix with the key vocabulary written in the left column. Students discuss the properties, features, characteristics, or elements that represent the topic and list these horizontally on the top axis. Encourage students to craft their own features to clarify word relationships.

Suggested Teacher Talk: *Think about these words and how they are associated. What information would you use to support the view of how these words are related?*

3. Prior to reading the text, students collaborate in pairs or as small groups or work independently to record and discuss their predictions of the relationships between the keywords and features. For each key concept on the left axis of the matrix, students can use a plus (+) or minus (–) as they are reading to indicate the presence or absence of a particular feature. Or they can use a Likert scale, using numbers (0–5) rather than symbols, to represent the degree to which the key concept relates to the feature.

4. Examine how this grid serves as a thinking tool to elicit students' prior knowledge, support critical thinking during reading, and guide reflection of learning after reading. During the process, students may add keywords to the left column as their understanding of the topic deepens.

5. Prompt students to articulate their reasoning for their responses by identifying terminology or features that remain uncertain. Direct students to revisit the text and to reflect on the vocabulary terminology and how the words are used in the text.

6. After they have read the text selection, guide students toward reflective dialogue, and synthesize and communicate group responses on a class chart. Support students to think critically, focusing on the associations between the key concepts and identified features.

Motivation/Engagement: *Intrapersonal.* Students can modify any portion of their matrix as needed to reflect new learning and capture this learning in a written summary in their notebooks, vocabulary journals, or through a secure electronic form of communication (e.g., blog).

Suggested Teacher Talk: *What information would you use to support and justify your view of how these words are related?*

Fusion

Vocabulary: Associating

Purpose: To link words and fuse ideas by forming a visual representation of the meaning of words and how they relate

Multiple Intelligences: Visual/spatial, verbal/linguistic, interpersonal, intrapersonal

Materials: Vocabulary words from text, chart paper or visual projection device

Procedure:

1. Select a content-related topic or concept based on what the class is studying. Initiate a discussion about the topic or concept to determine categories that support it through associations of class (categories of characteristics that describe the concept), property (attributes that define the concept), or examples (exemplars of the concept).

2. As a whole group, list words around the concepts or categories that relate to the chosen topic or concept. Display generated words on chart paper, with a visual projection device, or on a chalkboard.

3. Demonstrate how to categorize these brainstormed words by creating clusters under broader categories. Construct examples that demonstrate the word in the center of an oval and theorize how the words are fused together. This visual representation is a graphic word organizer called a Semantic Word Map (Heimlich & Pittelman, 1986) and demonstrates understanding of the words.

Suggested Teacher Talk: *How does the visual representation help you to connect and generate meaning of the word(s)?*

4. After creating the class Semantic Word Map as a visual representation, have students read content-related text and, when they encounter one of the words in the map, record it in their vocabulary journals along with how it was categorized in the text.

Motivation/Engagement: *Logical/mathematical.* To move from convergent to divergent thinking, have students use a form of a Capsule Vocabulary (Crist, 1975; Irwin, 1991). Present six to eight topically related vocabulary words one at a time with a brief discussion. These words may also be placed in a real capsule container and pulled out one at a time or displayed for all to see the words. Pairs engage in conversational dialogue using the capsule vocabulary and check off words as they use them in their conversations. Pairs can form teams with other pairs to compose a paper on the common topic using as many of the capsule words as they can.

Academic Word Wall

Academic Word Wall in the Classroom:

Vocabulary: Associating

Joni Olson, a high school English teacher, supports her students in making word associations by applying the Academic Word Wall technique before, during, and after a unit on modern fiction. She shared that many of her students were unfamiliar with the many historical events and vocabulary that defined the period. To initiate the Academic Word Wall, she selected key concepts or historical events and assigned one to each group (e.g., The Jazz Age, Popular Culture). Groups read the background provided in the textbook and were provided access to laptop computers for further Internet research. They created a word picture poster with important details that defined their historical event or vocabulary term. Mrs. Olson was pleased with the level of discussion and the evidence of understanding: "While reading our [modern fiction] stories, my students could refer to our Academic Word Wall when they had trouble remembering specific concepts, ideas, or events relating in our stories." Figure 5.3 shows one student's contribution to the Academic Word Wall.

Purpose: To provide visual clues for interacting with subject-specific concepts

Multiple Intelligences: Visual/spatial, logical/mathematical, bodily/kinesthetic

Materials: Word Relationships reproducible (for Motivation/Engagement activity; see Appendix), chart paper, 3-by-5-inch cards, markers

Procedure:

1. Select vocabulary essential for understanding the content theme or topic of study. Present the vocabulary in the context in which students will encounter it in their reading and apply it through discussion and writing. Using markers, add four or five key terms on 3-by-5-inch cards per week to the same visual display area throughout the study to encourage students to use the Word Wall as a learning tool.

2. On chart paper, students can elaborate by defining and creating a visual representation of the word to clarify meaning.

FIGURE 5.3. Student Work for a High School Class Academic Word Wall

3. Add vocabulary in an organized display; avoid overcrowding the Word Wall. Remove words, maintain some key vocabulary, or revisit concepts as the unit progresses. Words can be presented alphabetically or organized by themes or features, such as genres or historical movements in literature or history (e.g., transcendentalism, progressive movement).

4. Use the Word Wall as a brief (approximately 5 minutes) lesson introduction to link to prior learning, to use as a reflection piece at the end of class, or to further develop it as a vocabulary focus lesson. Use the Academic Word Wall vocabulary during reading, enabling students to interact and actively engage in discussions and processes to synthesize key terminology.

Motivation/Engagement: *Interpersonal.* Students can work in pairs or small groups to articulate, cluster, and identify similarities and differences among words. Use the Word Relationships reproducible as a "thinking map" (Hyerle, 2004) graphic word organizer to promote higher order reasoning. Ask students to choose several words from the word wall and record them on the graphic word organizer. Using the Word Relationships reproducible as a guide, students record descriptors, attributes, words, and phrases about how the two chosen words chosen. On the outer circles, students note attributes that are only specific for the particular word.

Vocabulary Strategy: Contextualizing

The contextualizing strategy allows readers to increase their vocabulary and extend comprehension by using the context that surrounds an unknown word, or *challenged word*. Using *context* is one of the most widely recommended vocabulary strategies (Graves, 2007). Readers use the various *cueing systems* as well as context *clue-glue words* as tools to derive meaning of an unknown word. Context clue-glue words can include categories such as definition words (e.g., *means, is, defines*), synonym words (e.g., *like, as if, same as*), or cause-and-effect words (e.g., *because, due to, consequently*). A study by Baumann, Font, Edwards, and Boland (2005) reveals how middle school students were able to use both linguistic and nonlinguistic information to unlock the meanings of unfamiliar words.

There is a discovery element that transpires as readers use surrounding information within the text to make predictions and that brings meaning to an unfamiliar word. The ability to make an inference or use the *clues* around the unknown word allows readers to take an *inquisitive stance* toward word meaning (Ellery, 2009; Greenwood & Flanigan, 2007; Nelson, 2008; Tierney & Readence, 2005). Taking an inquisitive stance permits readers to be active (productive), rather than passive (receptive), in the discovery of new words.

Key Vocabulary for Contextualizing

- Challenged Word: an unfamiliar or unknown word that leads the reader to doubt or question meaning in context

- Clues: hints or indications that support the understanding of an unknown word

- Clue-Glue Words: words from syntactic categories (e.g., definition, synonym, antonym) that help make the meaning for the unknown word stick

- Context: text that surrounds a word or passage

- Cueing Systems: self-extending systems built into the structure and patterns of the English language, which readers use to comprehend text. These sets of cues include how language is structured (syntax), the meaning of words (semantics), letter–sound correspondence (graphophonics), and determining the author's intent through the reader's metacognitive process (pragmatics).

- Inquisitive Stance: analytical position toward the search for the unknown words meaning

Assessment for Contextualizing

Use the following behaviors as a guide as you assess students' abilities to contextualize. Do students exhibit these behaviors never, rarely, often, or always?

☐ Predicts and verifies omitted words using surrounding context

☐ Uses background knowledge to examine and verify word meaning

☐ Cross-checks the meaning of a challenged word by using multiple cueing systems

Teacher Talk: Statements, Questions, and Prompts for Contextualizing

The following are suggestions for teacher talk that encourages readers to think strategically as they employ the contextualizing strategy. Try using some of these statements, questions, and prompts with your students as you work through the techniques in the following section. They are aligned with Bloom's taxonomy and Webb's DOK levels.

Level of Thinking	Teacher Talk
Creating Extended Thinking	• What would happen if you tried the new meaning of the word you chose in place of the word in the sentence? Does the word choice make sense given your understanding of the text?
Evaluating Strategic Thinking	• How would you justify the determination of the meaning of the challenged word? • Explain how you determined the meaning of the unknown word.

Analyzing Strategic Thinking	• What word would be used to signal that an opposite, contrasting thought is occurring? • After examining the clues (words within the sentence that supported your understanding of the unknown word), distinguish how you used the word in context (definition, cause and effect, opposite).
Applying Skill/Concept	• What clues in the sentence helped you figure out the word? • Look at the omitted word in the sentence. What word do you think best completes the sentence? Why? • Does the word look and sound correct for the English language? Does it make sense in the text?
Understanding Skill/Concept	• When you come to a word that you do not know, explain how you use context clues to determine the meaning of the unknown word. • What do you know about the word _____ based on how it was used in this sentence?
Remembering Recall	• What is a context clue? • Explain what it means for a word to have multiple meanings.

Techniques for Contextualizing

Content Multiple Meaning

Purpose: To understand how the meaning of a content word may vary depending on the content area in which it is used

Multiple Intelligences: Visual/spatial, verbal/linguistic, interpersonal, intrapersonal

Materials: Multiple-meaning words from content area text, chart, index cards, computers, vocabulary journals

Procedure:

1. Select content vocabulary with multiple meanings to demonstrate how the content area in which a word is used can change the meaning of the word.

2. Write the selected words on index cards and write a specific content area after each word. For example, one card will have the word *range* followed by the content area of *mathematics*. Another index card will have the same word, *range*, followed by *music*.

3. Distribute cards to student teams and ask them to create a sentence and illustration using their word in the content area in which it is presented.

Suggested Teacher Talk: *Think about the meaning of the word in the specific content area. Construct a sentence using the word to show the word's content meaning.* (Students may use any available print or online resources and their own background knowledge.)

4. Teams will determine a way to change their voice on the chosen word prior to reading the sentence aloud to the class (e.g., whisper, declarative, whimsical). Have the teams share out their created sentences to the whole group, changing their voices on the selected words and omitting the name of the content area.

5. Instruct the rest of the class to listen for the chosen word and then think about the context that surrounds the word and how the sentence was spoken to reveal the content area meaning. Display the word, content area, and meaning on a three-column chart.

6. Have the corresponding team then share how the same word may be used in a different content area.

7. Have students record the words in their vocabulary journals and brainstorm other terms that have multiple meaning across disciplines.

Motivation/Engagement: *Musical/rhythmic.* Have the students fold a piece of paper in half. On the left side of the fold, write a multiple-meaning word and create riddles, lyrics, or raps using context clues to define each meaning. On the right side of the fold, the students will illustrate the riddles, lyrics, or raps. Students reveal the answer on the back of the paper.

Inferring Word Meaning

Vocabulary: Contextualizing

Purpose: To use text clues to formulate evidence-based inferences and construct word meanings

Multiple Intelligences: Visual/spatial, verbal/linguistic, bodily/kinesthetic, interpersonal

Materials: Challenged Word Guide reproducible (see Appendix), texts, visual projection device, copies of text excerpt, or both

Procedure:

1. Use content area text excerpts that support contextualizing to practice making inferences. Students work independently to highlight or place a sticky note next to unfamiliar, or "challenged," words or phrases. Students predict the meaning of each challenged word or phrase and record the words and phrases and their predictions in a vocabulary journal or notebook.

2. Arrange students in small groups or pairs to share their list of challenged words and their initial prediction of the meaning of each word or phrase.

3. Model the process for constructing and using the Challenged Word Guide. This guide is a three-column graphic organizer. Students record words or phrases that are unclear in the first column. In the second column, they write what they think the word means. In the third column, they list the context clue words.

4. Groups select three or four words to explore and formulate definitions. Each group will use the guide for sharing their challenged words and phrases, inferred meanings, and author's clues that helped predict the meaning.

Suggested Teacher Talk: *What do you know about the challenged word or phrase based on how it was used in the sentence? What clues are in the rest of the sentence that helped you figure out the meaning of word or phrase?*

5. On chart paper or with electronic media, groups present their findings to the whole class. Students are encouraged to note any additional terms to their list in their vocabulary notebooks or journals.

Motivation/Engagement: *Musical/rhythmic.* Encourage students to use multiple representations to present their inferences (e.g., illustrations, pictures clues, musical renderings, drama, pantomime). Students can capture their words on 3-by-5-inch note cards and display them on Academic Word Walls (see the Academic Word Wall technique in the Associating section).

Suggested Teacher Talk: *How would you justify your determination of the meaning of the challenged words or phrases? Do the words or phrases make sense and lead to understanding?*

Context Complex Clues

Purpose: To use context clues to analyze the meaning of an unfamiliar word

Multiple Intelligences: Visual/spatial, verbal/linguistic, interpersonal

Materials: Types of Context Complex Clues reproducible (see Appendix), Clue-Glue Word Cards reproducible (see Appendix), text, notebooks, magnifying glass, poster chart paper

Procedure:

1. Using text from a specific content area, select several words to examine for meaning.

2. Create a large chart of the different types of context complex clues, or copy or enlarge the Types of Context Complex Clues reproducible (Ellery, 2009). Reproduce and cut the Clue-Glue Word Cards.

3. Distribute the Clue-Glue Word Cards to student volunteers. Display and read a sentence or sentences that use one of the chosen content words and highlight the word. Have students give predictions about the meaning of the highlighted word and write their predictions in their notebooks.

Suggested Teacher Talk: *Think about the sentence and the unfamiliar word. What do you think the word means based on the surrounding words?*

4. Remind the students that texts often have clues called *context clues* that hint at a word's meaning. Explain that these clues help "stick" the meaning of the unfamiliar word, and therefore the clues are called the "glue" word or words.

5. Ask the students to search the sentence(s) to determine if their Clue-Glue Word is within the sentence(s).

6. Ask the students to think about the types of Context Complex Clues and identify which kind of context clue the author used to "stick" the meaning. Place the Clue-Glue Word under the correct category type. Chart these words as Clue-Glue Words for each category of contextual clues.

Suggested Teacher Talk: *What Clue-Glue Words within the sentence help support the meaning of _____? (Discuss what clues in the sentence help convey the meaning of the word.)*

7. Continue with several more sentences, each time having a different volunteer identify the Clue-Glue Word.

Suggested Teacher Talk: *How did the author help you understand new words?*

Motivation/Engagement: *Intrapersonal.* Have students record unfamiliar words from other coursework and from their independent reading to transfer the learning into other disciplines. As needed, hold up the magnifying glass as a visual representation of the process to connect students with the concept. Those students holding the Clue-Glue Word share the word that is within the chosen sentence(s).

Inquisitive Stance

Vocabulary: Contextualizing

Purpose: To use cueing systems and context clues to predict an omitted word and reflect on word's meaning by using a semantic gradient

Multiple Intelligences: Visual/spatial, verbal/linguistic, logical/mathematical, interpersonal

Materials: Semantic Gradient reproducible (see Appendix); content text passage(s), sticky notes, visual projection device, student vocabulary notebooks or journals

Procedure:

1. Select an engaging content passage and display it on a visual projection device for easy viewing. Determine several key vocabulary words to omit and place large sticky notes over the words. Think aloud to model and guide students in using context clues to craft thoughtful predictions of the omitted words.

Suggested Teacher Talk: *What word do you think best completes the sentence? Why? What clues are in the sentence that helped you figure out the word?*

2. Guide students to develop an analytical position as they reflect and share words that best complete the passages. Students investigate by using questions that support the cueing systems to move toward an inquisitive stance.

Suggested Teacher Talk: *Does the word look and sound correct for the English language? Does it make sense in the text?*

FIGURE 5.4. Sample Semantic Gradients

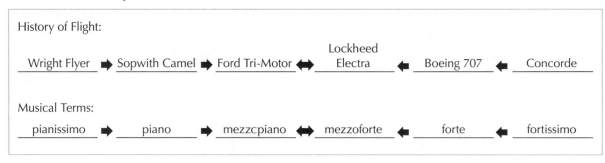

3. On sticky notes or chart paper, record the students' predictions of the omitted words.

4. As students finish generating their replacements words, peel back the sticky note from the first omitted word to allow students to view a portion of the word. Give students an opportunity to modify or change their predictions. Remove the sticky note completely, exposing the remainder of the missing word. Discuss with students how this technique guides them to cross-check, using various cueing systems as they reflect on meaning (semantic), letter–sound relationships (graphophonic), and the structure of the language (syntactic).

Suggested Teacher Talk: *Does your word choice make sense given your understanding of the text? Explain what cueing system(s) you used to determine the meaning of the unknown word.*

Motivation/Engagement: *Intrapersonal.* Using the words that students generated to complete the passage, explain that words can be connected to one another in different ways. Two ways are by degree and by order. Display the Semantic Gradient reproducible (see Appendix; Blachowicz & Fisher, 2006; Ellery, 2009; Greenwood & Flanigan, 2007) and have students determine where the words could be placed on a continuum. Encourage students to create their own semantic gradients by generating words from two ends of a continuum (see samples in Figure 5.4).

Vocabulary Strategy: Visualizing

Visualizing enables students to create an image representing the meaning of a word or concept. This *mental concept acquisition* also has been referred to as concept, mental, or mind imagery. Making *sensory connections* is the bond to meaning for visual learners. These learners know how to create an image or movie in their *mind's eye* as a vivid picture of the content or concept, thus creating a *content concept image*. When readers visualize, they are using their *spatial intelligence* (Silver, Strong, & Perini, 2001).

Research is proving that there needs to be interplay between verbal and visual information to activate different parts of the brain (Jensen, 2005; Ogle, 2000). According to the Greek philosopher Aristotle, "It is impossible to even think without a mental picture." Even Albert Einstein noted, "If I can't picture it, I can't understand it." For some learners in the content areas, educators need to provide opportunities for the use of picture books. Picture books allow adolescent readers a greater understanding of higher level concepts through lower level texts that support the various content areas (Hibbing & Rankin-Erickson, 2003).

Key Vocabulary for Visualizing

- Content Concept Image: a picture-like representation in the mind of a word that is heard or read and is related to specific content
- Mental Concept Acquisition: attainment of a mental representation of an idea, thought, or perception of a word
- Mind's Eye: visual perception in the mind; the ability to "see" things in the mind
- Sensory Connections: associations of word meanings using the senses
- Spatial Intelligence: the ability to think and learn the meaning of a word through shapes or arrangement of images in the mind

Assessment for Visualizing

Use the following behaviors as a guide as you assess students' abilities to visualize. Do students exhibit these behaviors never, rarely, often, or always?

- ☐ Imprints visual meaning by creating a mental image of a word
- ☐ Constructs sensory connection with the content
- ☐ Questions and hypothesizes the meaning of the image (its purpose and context)

Teacher Talk: Statements, Questions, and Prompts for Visualizing

The following are suggestions for teacher talk that encourages readers to think strategically as they employ the visualizing strategy. Try using some of these statements, questions, and prompts with your students as you work through the techniques in the following section. They are aligned with Bloom's taxonomy and Webb's DOK levels.

Level of Thinking	Teacher Talk
Creating Extended Thinking	• What can you combine to construct a model that would support your theory?
Evaluating Strategic Thinking	• Defend why you created the image you did to represent the content.

Analyzing Strategic Thinking	• Do the illustrations match what you imagined in your mind when you heard the story? • Which word goes with _____? Why does that word go with _____? • How does the example remind you of the word? • Why did you choose that movement or picture to represent the word _____?
Applying Skill/Concept	• Think about the word _____. What comes to mind that reminds you of the word? Describe what the word is like.
Understanding Skill/Concept	• Describe how your illustration helps you remember the new word.
Remembering Recall	• What do you see when you think of the word _____?

Techniques for Visualizing

Four Corners

Four Corners in the Classroom:

Bill Kebler, a middle school agritechnology instructor, applied the Four Corners vocabulary technique to support students in making word associations relating to technology concepts. His students seemed to have misconceptions and varied interpretations of the concept of "technology." Mr. Kebler shared that his students needed a solid understanding of relevant content vocabulary for speaking, writing, and successfully participating in technology competitions. He used the Four Corners technique with adaptations of the root word *way*, and supported students in crafting working definitions of terms such as *pathways* and *highways*. "Sometimes we assume students have a solid understanding of frequently used terms," said Mr. Kebler, "but areas of confusion become evident when they must apply these terms in writing and speaking."

Kristi Latture-Simpson, a high school science teacher in Bebe, Arkansas, supports her students in gaining a deeper understanding of essential physical science content vocabulary by applying the Four Corners technique (see student samples in Figure 5.5). She shared how she selected familiar vocabulary to model the Four Corners process and moved to more involved words that may have been more difficult to understand. Initially, some students struggled to visualize or illustrate a concept that was "not like," but Kristi continued to model and guide their responses: "I applied the process with the next section of the same chapter, and they loved it—presenting the most creative and real life responses!"

The Four Corners posters were displayed in the classroom as a learning tool so that students could see which words other classes selected and their descriptions. Kristi indicated

FIGURE 5.5. Sample Student Work for Four Corners

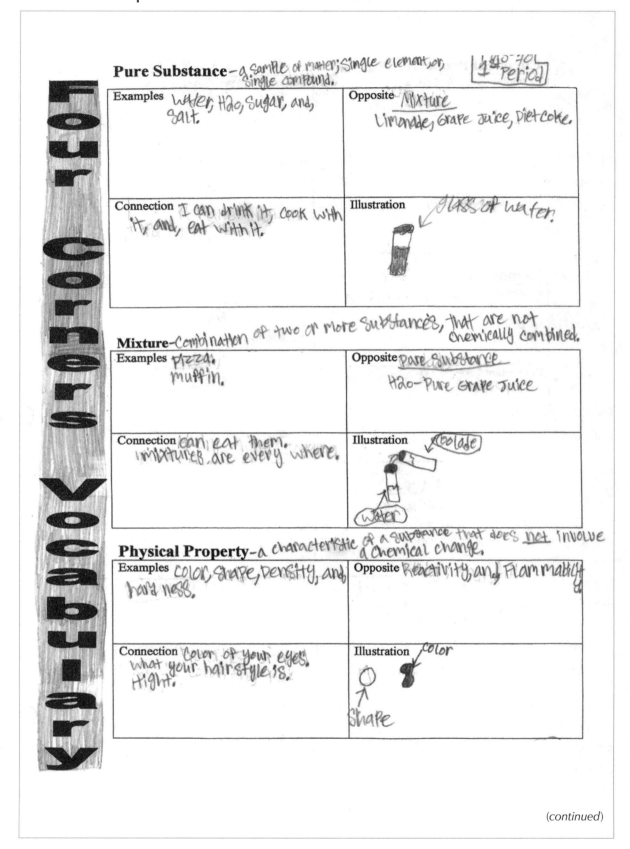

(continued)

FIGURE 5.5. Sample Student Work for Four Corners (Continued)

Chemical Property – Describes the ability too particulate a chemical reaction.

Examples Reactivity, and; Flammabilty.	Opposite Color, Density, Shape, and size.
Connection BonFire - Paint can explodes Sour milk.	Illustration Fire burning a car.

Homogeneous – uniform structure, or, composition throughout.

Examples Sugar water, and, salt water.	Opposite Fruit Salad, Heterogeneos.
Connection use salt water too kils Infect things.	Illustration Sugar and water

Heterogeneous – has dissimilar components.

Examples Fruit Salad. Hamburger.	Opposite Jello. Homogeneos.
Connection I eat fruit Salad. I eat Hamburgers.	Illustration Flour and water

(continued)

FIGURE 5.5. Sample Student Work for Four Corners (Continued)

Technology.

Definition: The application of science for practical uses.

Opposite: Taping two objects together.

Connection: Disassemble an electronic and put is back together to understand how it works and how it is made.

Picture: speakers

Disc changer

Science.

Definition: A search for explanations for things.

Opposite: Guessing or making up a story that could explain most things but not how

Connection: Find answers through rational proven explanation to understand complicated questions or quagmires.

Picture:

how this technique supported students of all ability levels to understand content vocabulary that they otherwise might have written down, defined, and then moved on. She said, "I could see by test scores that it increased the students' understanding of some very uncommon scientific terms that they will see again on state assessments."

Purpose: To visualize the meaning of a content-specific word

Multiple Intelligences: Visual/spatial, verbal/linguistic, bodily/kinesthetic, interpersonal

Materials: Four Corners reproducible (see Appendix), poster boards or large sticky note chart paper, pencils or markers

Procedure:

1. Present a content-specific word to the class. Divide the class into four teams. Give each team a poster board or a piece of large sticky chart paper.

2. Assign a different task card, adapted from the Frayer Model (Frayer, Frederick, & Klausmeier, 1969), to each team.

   - Task Card 1: Opposite—write what the word is NOT
   - Task Card 2: Example—write what the word IS like
   - Task Card 3: Connection—write a personal connection to the word
   - Task Card 4: Illustration—create a picture to demonstrate the word

3. Have the teams decide on a leader to share their findings. The team leaders take turns sharing while the rest of the students use their vocabulary notebooks or the Four Corners reproducible to record the presentations.

4. Display the four large posters in an area called the "concept wall." Arrange the posters to match the layout of the Four Corners reproducible, creating a large representation of the content-specific word or concept.

Sensory Scenery

Purpose: To use prior knowledge of a similar term to visualize an unknown word

Multiple Intelligences: Visual/spatial, verbal/linguistic, interpersonal, intrapersonal

Materials: Text, vocabulary notebook, chart paper

Procedure:

1. Have students think of a keyword that shares some common features to the new word (e.g., acoustically similar, but not necessarily similar in meaning), imagining it as a picture or creating a scene for the word.

2. Ask students to visualize a picture or scene that represents the meaning of the new word or information.

Vocabulary: Visualizing

Suggested Teacher Talk: *Try to visualize the meaning of the new word by creating an image that represents the meaning of the word.*

3. Have the students link the two pictures in their minds and share their creations with a partner.

Suggested Teacher Talk: *What do you see when you think of the word _____?*

4. Revisit the literature and highlight the words the students are studying. Students create sensory scenery in their vocabulary journals by illustrating the new words, capturing what they may see, hear, smell, taste, or touch when associating the words to their scenery.

Mind's Eye

Purpose: To use visual imagery to make meaning in your mind and to hypothesize the purpose and context of key concepts

Multiple Intelligences: Visual/spatial, verbal/linguistic, interpersonal, intrapersonal, naturalistic/environmental

Materials: Content text, illustrations, sketches, photographs, electronic graphic imagery; Optional: Word Splash reproducible (see Appendix), visual projection device, appropriate movie clips

Procedure:

1. Select a print or electronic text with a nonlinguistic representation (graphic) related to the current theme or content. Display only the graphic and ask students to reflect on what they see and to describe the picture. Encourage students to share their ideas with a partner.

2. Read aloud a portion of the text that correlates with the picture and guide students to make predictions (hypothesize) the possible thoughts, ideas, events, and problems associated with the picture or scene.

Suggested Teacher Talk: *How do the illustrations match what you imagined in your mind when you heard an excerpt of the story or text?*

3. Use a Word Splash (see the reproducible in the Appendix for an example; distribute the reproducible if desired) and ask students to brainstorm additional vocabulary that relates to the characters, setting, time period, and actions from the picture or graphic. Capture, or "splash," these ideas on chart paper, whiteboard, electronically, or on the reproducible.

4. Select two or three key concepts from the Word Splash or present other key concepts that are essential for the understanding the theme or unit. Ask students to close their eyes and create a mental image of the terms.

Suggested Teacher Talk: *Think about the word _____. What comes to mind that reminds you of the word(s) presented?*

5. In pairs, students will infer what they think will happen next in the text from the scene or graphic. Have students share ideas in whole group, making connections to the vocabulary from the Word Splash and other key concepts.

Motivation/Engagement: *Logical/mathematical.* View appropriate content-related movies clips without sound. Ask students to predict or hypothesize possible dialogue and vocabulary to go with the silent movie. Show the movie clip again, this time with sound. Students compare and contrast their predictions with the actual dialogue and vocabulary.

Suggested Teacher Talk: *Defend why you created the image and predictions you did to represent the content.*

Mind Maps

**Vocabulary:
Visualizing**

Purpose: To structure vocabulary networks and make visual connections between words

Multiple Intelligences: Visual/spatial, verbal/linguistic, interpersonal, intrapersonal

Materials: Content text, visual projection device or chart paper

Procedure:

1. Display a list of content-related words on the whiteboard, chart paper, or electronic media. Allow students an opportunity to reflect on their level of knowledge of the words. Use a two-minute focused dialogue for students to share their understanding of the words.

Suggested Teacher Talk: *Think about a chosen word from the generated list. What comes to mind that reminds you of the word? Reflect on your level of understanding of the word and describe what the word is like.*

2. For the whole group, model, using a think-aloud, one possible way to organize the words by creating a visual map.

3. Encourage students to generate a mental picture to visualize the connections between the focus words. Students organize the words in a Mind Map and then compare ideas on how they have grouped words and related them.

4. In pairs or small groups, students share their Mind Maps.

Motivation/Engagement: *Logical/mathematical.* Use this technique as a tool in the planning stage for writing, as students can structure ideas and discuss how they are related.

Vocabulary Strategy: Personalizing

Students use personalizing as a vocabulary strategy that increases a sense of ownership of a word. To support students in creating ownership, educators need to provide definition and context as well as multiple exposures, and use discussion (Stahl & Nagy, 2006). This ownership enables readers to bring their thinking about the usage of a word to an awareness level known as *word consciousness*. This level of engaging with a word to an application level personalizes word learning in verbal and written form. Personalizing words to a word-conscious level allows the reader to know the subtleties of word meaning and gives power to words (Graves, Juel, & Graves, 1998; Graves & Watts-Taffe, 2008).

Content-specific vocabulary is difficult for some readers because of the limited frequency with which they encounter the words in context. Therefore, it is vital for content area educators to create *word tapestries* of their content vocabulary through incidental learning. "In promoting students' *incidental word learning* through reading, considerations include recognizing the importance of *wide reading*, helping students select books that will promote vocabulary growth, and facilitating and encouraging their reading widely" (Graves, 2006, p. 40; emphases added). Wide reading incorporates a vast sampling of *genre jive* in the various content areas, enabling the readers to connect and personalize their word awareness while reading.

Key Vocabulary for Personalizing

- Genre Jive: categorizing words by specific genre

- Incidental Word Learning: secondary learning of word meaning resulting from exposure to word choices through a variety of contexts, such as conversations, movies, music, and literature

- Wide Reading: the reading of a plethora of text independently, exposing readers to more words, exposing word meaning in contexts, and expanding readers' background knowledge of words

- Word Consciousness: awareness, interest in, and ownership or personalization of words read and used, with a sense of enjoyment and engagement

- Word Tapestry: an intricate design of meaningful language made by weaving words spoken and read

Assessment for Personalizing

Use the following behaviors as a guide as you assess students' abilities to personalize. Do students exhibit these behaviors never, rarely, often, or always?

- ☐ Gains ownership of words by applying new words in everyday conversations
- ☐ Indicates levels of knowledge of words
- ☐ Identifies characteristics of words in various genres

Teacher Talk: Statements, Questions, and Prompts for Personalizing

The following are suggestions for teacher talk that encourages readers to think strategically as they employ the personalizing strategy. Try using some of these statements, questions, and

prompts with your students as you work through the techniques in the following section. They are aligned with Bloom's taxonomy and Webb's DOK levels.

Level of Thinking	Teacher Talk
Creating Extended Thinking	• How have you used some words from your vocabulary journals or word lists in your everyday conversation?
Evaluating Strategic Thinking	• Rate the word according to how much you know about the word. • Do you feel confident to use the word _____ in a conversation or in your writing? Why? Why not? • How did your word choice affect the other students' understanding of your journal entry? • What pattern do you notice the author using for his or her word choice?
Analyzing Strategic Thinking	• How did being aware of one word today help you to learn about that word? • Why are these words interesting to you? • In what genre would you most likely find these words?
Applying Skill/Concept	• What did you do to personalize the word? • How often did you use your chosen word in your journal writing?
Understanding Skill/Concept	• Tell about some interesting words you are encountering while you are reading. Have you used these words before in your own speaking or writing?
Remembering Recall	• What do you know about the word _____? • What kinds of words are common to this specific genre?

Techniques for Personalizing

Knowledge Rating

Purpose: To identify the level of knowledge of a word by having the students independently rate how well they know the concept or word

Multiple Intelligences: Visual/spatial, verbal/linguistic, interpersonal, intrapersonal, logical/mathematical

Materials: Content text, student vocabulary notebooks or journals

Procedure:

1. Determine words related to the content area and create a knowledge rating chart using a number system (e.g., 1 = *Never have seen the word*, 2 = *Not sure what this word means*, 3 = *Can define the word and use it*). Knowledge rating (Blachowicz, 1986) encourages students to think metacognitively about their conceptual background for each word being introduced.

2. Have students analyze their familiarity with the chosen words as a prereading strategy. Ask them to rate their knowledge of the meaning of each word by placing a check mark beside their level of knowledge on the knowledge rating chart you created.

Suggested Teacher Talk: *Try to rate the word according to how much you know about it: 1 means "I don't know anything (haven't seen or heard the word before)," 2 means "I have heard or seen this word (not sure what the word means)," 3 means "I know this word well (can define the word and use it in an intelligent "showing" sentence)."*

3. If the student is familiar with the word, a short definition is written in the column in the student's own language. Discuss some of the preliminary predictions about the words.

4. Create a class tally of how many students actually know each word and select words to focus on during the upcoming reading of the text. This will give an overall picture of those that have the vocabulary word at expressive knowledge (can communicate the meaning) versus receptive knowledge (recognize the word only).

5. Students skim the text to locate the words in context. After they read, have students reflect on their rating matrix and determine whether their knowledge of certain words changed or was confirmed. Have students place an *X* in the appropriate column of the matrix to represent any changes.

6. Ask students to keep their rating charts in a personal vocabulary log and review them periodically, making adjustments on words that are becoming more familiar to them. Encourage them to use these terms in the expressive oral and written work with partners as they study the concepts.

7. Reread the text, and have students listen for the new words they are studying and think about how they are used in context.

Genre Jive

Purpose: To identify similarities and differences among vocabulary words within genres

Multiple Intelligences: Visual/spatial, verbal/linguistic

Materials: Texts in a variety of genres, chart, materials for creative writing, highlighters

Procedure:

1. Locate a variety of genre "jive" words—words that reflect a specific genre (Ellery, 2009) and content area (see Figure 5.6 for examples).

FIGURE 5.6. Examples of Genre Jive Words

Genre	Vocabulary Words and Phrases
Science	Encounter, discovery, scientific
Mystery	Suspense, classified, investigate, clue
Fable	Teaching a lesson, moral, responsibility

2. During this genre study, ask students to continue adding to a class chart of specific vocabulary words that correlate with each particular genre and content area being studied.

Suggested Teacher Talk: *What kinds of words did you notice that are common in the specific genre?*

3. Have students frequently discuss the similarities and differences among the vocabulary words within the various genres.

Suggested Teacher Talk: *In what genre would you most likely find these words?*

Motivation/Engagement: *Interpersonal.* Using the genre chart, have students select a genre and create a writing piece using at least 10 words that strongly indicate their genre choice. Have partners read the writing, identify the chosen genre, and highlight the words that correlate with the genre.

Word Tech

Purpose: To become powerful in applying words using technology

Multiple Intelligences: Visual/spatial, verbal/linguistic, bodily/kinesthetic

Materials: Computers, iPhones, or some form of online capability

Procedure:

1. Students use vocabulary websites to apply meaning of words in a plethora of ways:

- Visualthesaurus.com or visuwords.com—these are interactive dictionaries and thesauruses that create word maps and produce diagrams that demonstrate word meaning and associations with other words or concepts

- OneLook.com—a search engine for a variety of online dictionaries

- Wordsmith.org—a site that features a daily word with its meaning, etymology, usage, and pronunciation; it also offers anagrams, acronyms, and dictionary and thesaurus usage

- Punoftheday.com—an online program that allows students to search for specific words to find humorous puns related to the word, or twists on the word's meaning or sound

Vocabulary Strategy: Referencing

Referencing is a strategy that allows readers to use *resources* to determine the meaning of a word. This strategy requires more than just looking up the definition of a word in the dictionary. "Definitions alone can lead to only a relatively superficial level of word knowledge. By itself, looking up words in a dictionary or memorizing definitions does not reliably improve reading comprehension" (Nagy, 1988, p. 5). Referencing directs the student to a source for help or information when encountering unknown words.

Instructing students on how to reference the meaning of words for the appropriate context is key. When readers activate their ability to reference a word, they are using an indicator that orients them to bring clarification and meaning. These *resource indicators* can be in forms such as a dictionary, glossary, online *search engines*, or a thesaurus. "To make *deriving the meaning* from the dictionary definitions most effective, it needs to be modeled for students and practiced in a scaffolded way" (Beck et al., 2008, p. 47). The ability to use these resources effectively requires readers to understand the various elements involved with a particular resource reference (e.g., dictionary parts).

Key Vocabulary for Referencing

- Deriving Meaning: deducing the meaning from the resources provided

- Resource Indicator: a print or online resource that provides quantified information to obtain the meaning of a word

- Resources: sources of help for determining the meaning of a word

- Search Engine: a Web-based software program that searches for sites based on specific keywords and returns a list of choices connected to the keyword

Assessment for Referencing

Use the following behaviors as a guide as you assess students' abilities to reference. Do students exhibit these behaviors never, rarely, often, or always?

- ☐ Analyzes resource indicators and determines their purpose for bringing meaning to a word

- ☐ Uses glossaries, dictionaries, and thesauruses to determine meaning of words

- ☐ Selects meaning of a word that best supports the use of the word in context

Teacher Talk: Statements, Questions, and Prompts for Referencing

The following are suggestions for teacher talk that encourages readers to think strategically as they employ the referencing strategy. Try using some of these statements, questions, and

prompts with your students as you work through the techniques in the following section. They are aligned with Bloom's taxonomy and Webb's DOK levels.

Level of Thinking	Teacher Talk
Creating Extended Thinking	• Formulate a definition of the word based on how it is used in context. Elaborate on the reason for your definition of the word.
Evaluating Strategic Thinking	• How can you prove the word's meaning? • How does the communication tool used determine the degree of information received?
Analyzing Strategic Thinking	• Discuss the various meanings of the word _____. Describe which meaning best represents the identified word and why? • Analyze which search engine provided the best response to your search and why.
Applying Skill/Concept	• Think about the word _____. Which word means _____? How did you find the meaning for the word? What keywords did you use to narrow your search on the Web search engine?
Understanding Skill/Concept	• How did the dictionary help you to figure out the word?
Remembering Recall	• What feature helps you to know if a word will be in the glossary?

Techniques for Referencing

Start Your Engines

Purpose: To navigate online search engines to find meanings of words

Multiple Intelligences: Visual/spatial, verbal/linguistic, bodily/kinesthetic

Materials: Web-based technology, variety of search engines

Procedure:

1. Examine the use of keywords and phrases as a starting point that might lead to necessary topical information. Explain how online search engines deliver multiple results from technology and that the information might be found in any one of the results that come up after a keyword or phrase search.

Suggested Teacher Talk: *How does the communication tool you used determine the degree of information received?*

2. Investigate the various types of search engines and their functions (e.g., page rank, statistic bar, dictionary definitions, search results). Below are a few recommended search engines for keyword vocabulary development:

- Googlewonderwheel.com—a graphical representation of related search items
- Visuwords.com—a site that creates a word map of connections and word families
- Eyeplorer.com—a colorful wheel that arranges topics by categories
- Shahi (blachan.com/shahi/)—a visual dictionary that combines wiktionary.org content with flickr.com images

3. Have students select three search engines and try out the same topical search in each.

Suggested Teacher Talk: *Describe which search engine provided the best response to your search and why. What keywords did you use to narrow your search?*

4. Students record in the vocabulary journal the keyword or phrase that supported their connection to the necessary information.

Resource Course

Vocabulary: Referencing

Purpose: To effectively use the glossary and thesaurus to analyze content vocabulary

Multiple Intelligences: Verbal/linguistic, interpersonal

Materials: Content text with glossary, text selection with key vocabulary emphasized typographically (e.g., bold, italics, color), dictionary, thesaurus, sticky notes, markers, student notebooks or journals

Procedure:

1. Prior to reading a content text, students can initiate their journey by skimming the selection and noting the text features that are used for emphasizing important vocabulary (e.g., bold print, italics, different colors). The emphasized terms often align with the word selections in the text glossary.

2. For the next steps on their journey, students work independently to select terms that are emphasized in the content text selection and brainstorm possible definitions, synonyms, and antonyms for each word. Students share their chosen vocabulary definition predictions with a partner.

3. Working in pairs, students confirm or modify their predictions through analysis of the words in a dictionary, glossary, or thesaurus. Students note the definitions (from the glossary or dictionary), synonyms, and antonyms on 3-by-5-inch cards or in vocabulary journals or notebooks. When applicable, encourage students to include a visual representation to enhance their understanding.

4. Wrap up the journey by leading students in a whole-group discussion about how the dictionary, glossary, and thesaurus support student learning and vocabulary understanding.

Suggested Teacher Talk: *How might these resource tools support the writing process?*

Motivation/Engagement: *Visual/spatial.* Encourage students to use online dictionary and thesaurus resources (e.g., www.dictionary.com, www.thesaurus.com, dictionary.cambridge .org). Use the Word-Net Wheel technique (see the Associating strategy in this chapter) as a tool for student application in organizing and displaying their dictionary or glossary definitions, synonyms, and antonyms.

Defining Moment

Purpose: To explore the dictionary features to sum up the meaning of a word

Multiple Intelligences: Verbal/linguistic, bodily/kinesthetic, interpersonal, intrapersonal

Materials: Defining Moment Feature Cards reproducible (see Appendix), Four Corners reproducible (see Appendix), dictionaries, technological support (e.g., online dictionary sources)

Procedure:

1. Preview content text and select essential academic vocabulary for students to explore for a deeper understanding.

2. Copy and distribute the Defining Moment Feature Cards (pronunciation, syllabication, parts of speech, etymology [history of the word], definitions, and synonyms).

3. Model the process for Defining Moment using a sample content word. Using a print or online dictionary, locate the sample word and read aloud each of the dictionary resource features noted on the Defining Moment Feature Cards. Select four of the cards as focus areas to create a Four Corners mode (see the Visualizing strategy in this chapter) on notebook paper or chart paper. Use a think-aloud to demonstrate how each feature provides the reader with a deeper understanding of the word.

4. Initially, assign each group one of the focus content vocabulary words. In table groups of four or five, students collaborate to distribute the Defining Moment Feature Cards (there are six cards, so some group members may need to present two cards to their group), and locate their focus word using a print or online dictionary resource. Students use the information on their assigned card(s) as a guide for sharing their word feature(s) with the group.

5. Groups will need to identify four of the Defining Moment Feature Cards that would support understanding of the focus vocabulary to create their Four Corners model. Encourage students to be creative by using diagrams, models, or illustrations to share their focus vocabulary term.

6. Each group presents their vocabulary word to the whole class. Display the groups' work in the classroom during the theme or unit of study to revisit key vocabulary.

7. Guide students in a reflective discussion on how the multiple features presented in a print or online dictionary support readers in extending their understanding beyond a definition.

Motivation/Engagement: *Visual/spatial.* Encourage students to self-select their Defining Moment vocabulary in the text. Deepen word associations by having students craft an acrostic poem using the letters from their word. An acrostic poem takes a word and uses each of its letters as the first letter of a line in the poem (see www.readwritethink.org, search on keywords "acrostic poem" for a selection of lessons).

Comprehension: Frontloading and Downloading

Activating and Connecting with **Read and Say**

Inquiring and Inferring with **Ripple Effect**

Determining Importance with **Highlighting the Highs**

Effective comprehension instruction supports learners in becoming purposeful and reflective readers who are in control of their own reading comprehension. According to Brassell and Rasinski (2008), "Comprehension occurs when a reader is able to act on, respond to, or transform the information that is present in written text in ways that it demonstrates understanding" (p. 18). However, the cognitive process of comprehension often eludes many secondary readers. In addition, educators may find comprehension instruction to be a mystery (Gill, 2008; Lenski & Lewis, 2008; Onofrey & Theurer, 2007).

Frontloading comprehension includes assessing, activating, and building a student's conceptual or procedural knowledge or both, which are necessary to successfully comprehend content text (Smith & Wilhelm, 2002). Before students begin reading, teachers set the stage for learning by motivating, setting purposes, and monitoring their students for the understanding of new content and use of new procedures or reading strategies. "Comprehension is contingent on the ability to draw upon your previous knowledge base to meet the author's expectations; so that you can understand what the author assumes will be new knowledge to most readers" (Buehl, 2009a, p. 15).

Comprehension strategies that are planned consciously, taught explicitly, and founded on motivating and engaging instruction may support students in actively using a repertoire of strategies (Caskey, 2008). Lapp and Fisher (2009) state, "The goal is to produce readers who can automatically deploy the cognitive strategies" (p. 4). Strategic readers "download" content information systematically for long-term retention and understanding. Downloading comprehension strategies focus on multiple exposures to text, critical thinking, determining importance, summarizing, and synthesizing. Comprehension strategies support students in transferring and transforming content learning into meaning.

The frontloading and downloading comprehension strategies and corresponding techniques detailed in this chapter are designed as a framework for teachers to use to support students in securing background knowledge and clarifying the purpose for a reading task. To effectively use the comprehension strategies and techniques presented in this chapter, ample time should be allotted for teacher modeling, student engagement, and scaffolding of learning. This goal is to structure instruction to support independent application and student ownership of learning.

Teachers can use the Motivation/Engagement section within many techniques as an additional means of motivating the whole learner and creating 21st-century secondary learners (refer to Chapter 1 for a description of the whole learner and to Figure 1.1 for an illustration of the composition of a 21st-century secondary learner). The Motivation/Engagement section allows for differentiation within the technique as needed to meet the needs of all learners. This section identifies and uses a multiple intelligence other than those that are highlighted in the main procedure of the technique.

Educators should use these comprehension strategies and techniques within the lesson planning and instructional process. However, it is essential to understand that these strategies and techniques are multifaceted and can be interchangeable within the components of lesson planning (before, during, and after instruction). The comprehension techniques support secondary learners to sustain independence as readers and acquire the reading strategies.

The following are the strategies and techniques in this chapter:

- Previewing: Text Traits, Constructing Structure, Skim and Scan, Implanting Vocabulary

- Activating and Connecting: Read and Say, Text/Concept Connections, Two-Column Entries

- Predicting: Initial Sentences, Passage/Concept Impressions, Prediction Boxes, Anticipation/Reaction Guide

- Inquiring and Inferring: Reflect on Questions, Authentic Questions (3Rs), Text Inquiry, Save the Last Word, Ripple Effect

- Determining Importance: Main Idea Wheel, Narrative and Nonfiction Pyramids, Highlighting the Highs

- Summarizing and Synthesizing: Diverge/Converge, Somebody Wanted But So, Get to the Point

Comprehension Strategy: Previewing

Previewing can set the stage for active reading by establishing a purpose. Data about adolescent readers from Graves and associates concur that previewing text before reading increases students' learning by a significant and impressive amount (Chen & Graves, 1995; Graves & Cooke, 1980; Graves, Cooke, & Laberge, 1983). Previewing enables students to *skim and scan* the potential text to determine the "why" for reading further. Previewing can create a desire and *mental hook* necessary to motivate students to read the text. This strategy is "beneficial when reading expository materials, because these texts often have explicitly marked structures (e.g., introduction, supporting details, conclusions, etc.) that help readers identify the goals of the reading" (McNamara, Ozuru, Best, & O'Reilly, 2007, p. 475). As a result of previewing, students use the *text traits* to engage them with the text and begin to discern the meaning of what they are reading. This *frontloading comprehension* process *constructs structures* to get their minds ready to read a particular type of unfamiliar text. Readers build their foundation of learning as they augment information they understand through their reading. Building background knowledge of unfamiliar vocabulary supports learners' academic achievement within specific content areas (Marzano, 2004). It is vital that teachers are cognizant of concepts in which students have little or no background knowledge so that they can build essential understandings through scaffolding previewing techniques (Fisher, Frey, & Lapp, 2009; Jensen & Nickelsen, 2008; Strickland et al., 2002).

Key Vocabulary for Previewing

- Construct Structure: to build foundational background knowledge

- Frontloading Comprehension: facilitating attention in the early stage of interacting with the text to motivate, set purpose, and prepare the readers prior to reading the text

- Mental Hook: a vivid mental image tied to something you will remember; an image to which you can attach a piece of information for recall

- Skim and Scan: to glance quickly (skim) to get the general idea of the text, and to peruse (scan) looking for specific details within the text

- Text Traits: text features, supports, and structures such as lists, headings, diagrams, and bold font

Assessment for Previewing

Use the following behaviors as a guide as you assess students' abilities to preview. Do students exhibit these behaviors never, rarely, often, or always?

☐ Augments background knowledge

☐ Uses text features and supports to preview purpose

☐ Applies text structures to determine purpose

Teacher Talk: Statements, Questions, and Prompts for Previewing

The following are suggestions for teacher talk that encourages readers to think strategically as they employ the previewing strategy. Try using some of these statements, questions, and prompts with your students as you work through the techniques in the following section. They are aligned with Bloom's taxonomy and Webb's DOK levels.

Level of Thinking	Teacher Talk
Creating 　Extended Thinking	• Reflect on the significance of the title. Create an alternative title. • Think about what comes to your mind when you hear the words or phrase in this heading, and propose and your own heading for this section. • How do the text supports help you question the author prior to reading?
Evaluating 　Strategic Thinking	• When you have finished reading, what new information might you have learned? How does this information align with what you have learned before? • Describe your purpose for reading this selection. • Would you consider this source to be a valid resource to help you extend your knowledge and reflect on the content? Justify your response. Why or why not?
Analyzing 　Strategic Thinking	• Think about what you read and reflect on this thought: "I have read other books by this author. I think this book will also be good because...." Explain your response. • What features help you when previewing the book?

	• Identify how you supported your thinking—with the text, background knowledge, or both.
	• Which details or clues from the selection did you use to frontload the content?
Applying Skill/Concept	• Think about the topic or concepts of this selection. Explain what you already know about this topic.
	• Read the title or opening paragraph, and name a book similar to this one.
	• What do you notice about the text's layout?
	• What are the signal words that may provide clues about what this text will explain?
Understanding Skill/Concept	• Think about what you read and reflect on this thought: "The title makes me think the book will be about…." Explain your response.
	• Think about what was read and reflect on this thought: "Perhaps the pictures will provide clues about…." Explain your response.
	• What does the text seem to be about?
	• How is the text structured?
Remembering Recall	• Finish these thoughts: "The illustrations help me to…."; "I noticed…."
	• What else do you notice from the picture or captions? What is the significance of the title?

Techniques for Previewing

Text Traits

Purpose: To identify and use text features, supports, and structures to help determine the purpose and organization of a text

Multiple Intelligences: Visual/spatial, verbal/linguistic, interpersonal

Materials: Text Traits reproducible (see Appendix), text

Procedure:

1. Preview specific text traits (Ellery, 2009) using the Text Traits reproducible to support the students' ability to anticipate what the text is about and discover the organizational structure.

Suggested Teacher Talk: *How is the text organized? What features help you when previewing the book?*

2. Have students work with a partner to investigate the various text traits.

Suggested Teacher Talk: *Which details or clues from the selection did you use to frontload the content?*

3. Have students pause throughout the reading to apply the text traits and explain how they support their understanding.

Motivation/Engagement: *Logical/mathematical.* Students create a preview guide or a scavenger hunt (Allen, 2004; Kane, 2007) to have other classmates explore, compare, and contrast the various text traits. Guide features may include text features, supports, or structures; purposes of text traits; title of book; type of genre; and page number.

Sample Preview Guide Questions:

1. Write the page number where you located an example of a political cartoon.

2. Find a chart that clarifies the data and explains reasoning.

3. Describe the gist of what you will be reading, as you peruse the table of contents.

Constructing Structure

Purpose: To generate and augment background knowledge to prepare to read for meaning

Multiple Intelligences: Visual/spatial, verbal/linguistic, intrapersonal

Materials: Constructing Structure Guide reproducible (see Appendix), print or online content text or both, highlighters or small sticky notes

Procedure:

1. Initiate the Constructing Structure process by identifying a nonfiction text or portions of texts that include examples of the author's use of text supports.

2. Guide the students to develop their Constructing Structure Guide. Students independently skim the title, illustrations, and headings to determine what they think they will learn from the selection. In notebooks or journals, students list three to five things they predict they will learn.

3. Encourage students to share their ideas with a partner.

Suggested Teacher Talk: *When you finish reading, what new information might you have learned? How does this information align with what you have learned before?*

4. Revisit the text, focusing students on subheadings, signal words, text layout, graphs, charts, and illustrations. After revisiting the text, students record the title, heading, subheadings, and other text supports in their Constructing Structure Guide or notebook.

Suggested Teacher Talk: *What do you notice about the text's layout? What are the signal words that may provide clues about what this text will explain?*

5. Guide the students to use the title, headings, and subheadings to create three prediction questions that they will try to answer while reading the text.

Suggested Teacher Talk: *How do the text supports help you question the author prior to reading?*

Motivation/Engagement: *Interpersonal.* Encourage students to work in groups to share their Constructing Structure Guides. As a whole group or in small groups, list, organize, and label categories of information students know about the topic and questions they would like to have answered.

Skim and Scan

Comprehension:
Previewing

Purpose: To process information before reading by looking for clues, searching for specific information, or reviewing information

Multiple Intelligences: Visual/spatial, verbal/linguistic, bodily/kinesthetic, interpersonal, intrapersonal

Materials: Print or online content text or both

Procedure:

1. Use an analogy of panning for gold to help students craft a mental image, or mental hook, to clarify the technique Skim and Scan. Gold panning involves sampling an area for evidence so prospectors might know where to dig deeper to recover more gold. During the California Gold Rush of the 1800s, prospectors would sample an area with their pan by scooping up soil or gravel from a stream bed into the pan and then shaking it to encourage the heavier gold to settle to the bottom of the pan. After skimming or sampling the stream bed, the prospectors then needed to dig deeper to look for nuggets of gold. It was a painstaking but beneficial task, as there is nothing like finding gold in the bottom of the pan! The strategy of previewing text is similar, as readers skim to capture the main ideas of a text and then scan to search for specific vocabulary, ideas, or topics that will help them get ready to read and take in more detailed and complex information.

2. Have students skim the content selection they are preparing to read and have them note their initial impressions.

Suggested Teacher Talk: *Move your eyes down the page. What specific words and phrases provide clues and help you figure out what you might learn from your reading? Readers may scan a resource to determine whether they think it will answer their questions.*

3. Explain to students that after initially skimming the text, you might decide to dig deeper and scan for specific information. Encourage students to scan the text supports, such as subheadings, diagrams, charts, graphs, and any other portions that provide clues, to help clarify the content of the text.

Suggested Teacher Talk: *How does the author use text traits such as numbers, letters, and transition words to develop your understanding? What other traits are evinced in the reading? These could be boldfaced words, italics, font style, color, and marginal notes. What strategies may be needed to comprehend this text?*

4. Discuss and record the varieties of accessible text that we use on a daily basis (e.g., electronic text, newspapers, magazines) and the benefits of Skim and Scan with various types of content text.

Motivation/Engagement: *Logical/mathematical.* Ask students to brainstorm possible content-specific research topics or essential questions. Model how to use Skim and Scan with various types of content text. Students can practice the Skim and Scan technique and identify multigenre resources that would help them gather information and evaluate and interpret findings to answer their research questions.

Suggested Teacher Talk: *Would you consider this source to be a valid resource to help you extend your knowledge and reflect on the content? Justify your response. Why or why not?*

Implanting Vocabulary

Comprehension: Previewing

Purpose: To identify and focus on the main idea by previewing, defining, and sorting key concepts

Multiple Intelligences: Verbal/linguistic, bodily/kinesthetic, interpersonal, intrapersonal

Materials: Content area text, note cards or multipurpose paper cut into strips

Procedure:

1. Select key concepts in advance of reading a content area text passage, or have students brainstorm words and phrases related to the central content theme or idea (e.g., for *democracy*, Merriam-Webster online [www.m-w.com] suggests *republic, self-rule,* and *self-government*). Note that the technique Implanting Vocabulary, an adaptation of Concept-Definition Sort (Kelly & Clausen-Grace, 2007), can be used in conjunction with Word Splash (see the technique Mind's Eye in Chapter 5, "Vocabulary").

Suggested Teacher Talk: *Think about the topic or concepts of this selection. Explain what you already know about this topic.*

2. Capture keywords and definitions on note cards or paper strips. Each concept is written on one card or paper strip and the definition on a separate card or paper strip. You may want to put students into small groups and assign three to five concepts to each group. The groups define their terms (using a context definition, glossary, or print or online dictionary) and record the definitions on the cards or paper strips.

3. Distribute the completed concept and definition cards. If student groups wrote the definitions, make sure groups get different terms they haven't seen at this point. Students

are encouraged to use prior knowledge and group discussion to match the concept with the appropriate definition.

4. Revisit key concepts to clarify any misconceptions, as these concepts will be encountered again through reading and class discussions.

Suggested Teacher Talk: *Confirm or modify your definitions during and after reading. How do the words connect with the content or area of study?*

Motivation/Engagement: *Visual/spatial* Secondary students can create unique descriptions of new vocabularies by brainstorming song lyrics or titles that describe the concept (e.g., *convene* = "We Gather Together"; *mobile* = "Movin' on Out"). Have students craft and share their descriptions of new vocabulary. Students can craft lyrical descriptions in small groups or as a whole class or can maintain individual notes in their vocabulary notebooks. Encourage students to support their descriptions with nonlinguistic visual supports.

Comprehension Strategy: Activating and Connecting

When readers activate *prior knowledge* they begin connecting to their *schema*, tapping into previous experiences and knowledge to discern the meaning of what they are reading (Harvey & Goudvis, 2000; McKeown, Beck, Sinatra, & Loxterman, 1992; Schallert, 1982; Schmidt & Patel, 1987; Spires & Donley, 1998). This frontloading process allows readers to evoke relevant thoughts and memories relating to the text: "When information is read in isolation and not connected to existing knowledge, it is forgotten and deemed unimportant. Calling on existing knowledge and experiences is crucial if readers are to assimilate new information" (Tovani, 2000, p. 64). According to Keene and Zimmermann (2007), students make *text-to-self*, *text-to-text*, and *text-to-world* connections. These connections can be made from all the text traits prior to reading (frontloading) from the text features and supports, during reading (processing), and after reading (downloading). Students can also make connections to key concepts in the content areas using this structure.

Key Vocabulary for Activating and Connecting

- Prior Knowledge: previous understanding about a subject that supports gaining new information

- Schema: knowledge in memory that relates incoming information to prior experiences aligned to concepts, beliefs, expectations, and processes; prior knowledge

- Text/concept-to-self: connections made between the reader's personal experiences and the text being read

- Text/concept-to-text: connections made between other texts previously read and the text being read
- Text/concept-to-world: connections made between something occurring in the world and the text being read

Assessment for Activating and Connecting

Use the following behaviors as a guide as you assess students' abilities to activate and connect. Do students exhibit these behaviors never, rarely, often, or always?

- ☐ Activates prior knowledge to connect with text
- ☐ Identifies text/concept connections to self prior to reading
- ☐ Examines text/concept connections to other text prior to reading
- ☐ Explores text/concept connections to world prior to reading

Teacher Talk: Statements, Questions, and Prompts for Activating and Connecting

The following are suggestions for teacher talk that encourages readers to think strategically as they employ the activating and connecting strategy. Try using some of these statements, questions, and prompts with your students as you work through the techniques in the following section. They are aligned with Bloom's taxonomy and Webb's DOK levels.

Level of Thinking	Teacher Talk
Creating Extended Thinking	• Brainstorm a list of what you think of when you hear the words _____ (prevocabulary words). • What do the words _____ mean to you?
Evaluating Strategic Thinking	• Prepare a case to present your view about _____. • Prioritize your knowledge about this subject.
Analyzing Strategic Thinking	• Reflect on the subject. What other content information or story do the text features or supports make you think about? What made that information or story so memorable?
Applying Skill/Concept	• What personal connection did you make when you were previewing the text? How are the events in the text traits related to your own experiences? What made the event so memorable? What are you reminded of as you preview this section?
Understanding Skill/Concept	• Read the title or heading to yourself and then tell me what you already know about any of the information.
Remembering Recall	• What comes to mind when you hear this topic?

Read and Say

Purpose: To construct meaning, self-monitor understanding, and make clear connections with complex content text resources

Multiple Intelligences: Verbal/linguistic, interpersonal, intrapersonal

Materials: Content text, highlighters or sticky notes

Procedure:

1. Students can work in groups of up to four to engage in the Read and Say process (Beers, 2003; Harste, Short, & Burke, 1988) by focusing and reflecting on what they are reading.

2. Small groups take turns reading a section, or "chunk," of text aloud. After one student reads aloud, the student to his or her right will respond using a text-to-self, text-to-text, or text-to-world connection. The student may also "say something" by making a prediction, asking a question, or summarizing.

Suggested Teacher Talk: *What puzzles you while reading? Predict what we will learn as we read the next section, or "chunk."*

3. Continue the process until groups have completed reading the text.

4. Debrief the process in a whole-group setting and continue the discussion, focusing on any challenging questions that surfaced during Read and Say.

Motivation/Engagement: *Visual/spatial.* Using nonlinguistic notes, encourage groups to capture and chart key ideas from the content reading passage. Groups can present their picture notes and post them in the room as a visual instructional tool.

Text/Concept Connections

Purpose: To make relevant connections between the text and self, text and another text, and text and world associations.

Multiple Intelligences: Verbal/linguistic, interpersonal, intrapersonal

Materials: Text/Concept Connections Prompts reproducible (see Appendix), content text, highlighters or sticky notes

Procedure:

1. Explain that a text/concept-to-self connection is made when something in the text or a concept reminds you of something in your own life. Use the Text/Concept Connections Prompts adapted from applying text connections (Ellery, 2009; Harvey & Goudvis, 2007; Keene & Zimmermann, 2007).

Comprehension: Activating and Connecting

Comprehension: Activating and Connecting

2. Using a think-aloud process, read aloud a few paragraphs from the content text or related text. Focus the students on "thinking" prompts, such as the following suggestions (also listed on the Text/Concept Connections Prompts reproducible):

Text/Concept-to-Self

- That is interesting to me because….

- This relates to my experiences….

- This reminds me of….

Text/Concept-to-Text/Concept

- The (character[s], setting, events) are similar to another text….

- This is (similar to, different from) another text I have read….

- This reminds me of another text that I have read….

Text/Concept-to-World

- This was significant in the real world….

- The reading related to the world around me….

- This text (compares, contrasts, or both) with current or historical world experiences….

3. Read the next section of the text together and have the students illustrate or write the events or information from the text on one half of a piece of paper and their personal connections on the other half.

Suggested Teacher Talk: *What made the event from the text so memorable? What are you reminded of as you preview this section?*

Motivation/Engagement: *Visual/spatial.* As they work on the Text/Concept Connections technique, students can work in groups of up to four and use the Read and Say technique structure (Beers, 2003; Harste et al., 1988) to help students focus and reflect on what they are reading. Students can refer to the posted Text/Concept Connections Prompts to support student discussion of the Read and Say.

Two-Column Entries

Purpose: To make connections to background knowledge, reflect, infer, and clarify misconceptions before reading

Multiple Intelligences: Visual/spatial, verbal/linguistic, interpersonal, intrapersonal

Materials: Paper, text

Procedure:

1. Have students divide a sheet of paper into two vertical columns by folding it lengthwise. Students will use the folded paper notes as a form of Double-Entry Journals (Buehl, 2001).

This process encourages students to be active thinkers as they read, to organize knowledge, and to review materials.

2. In the left column, have students take notes on specific information from the text. On the right side, have students record their personal reactions and connections to the information. The students can label the right column "This reminds me of…." Variations for the right column of a Two-Column Entries may include the following:

- Questioning: "I wonder…."
- Making inferences: "I figured out that…because…."
- Clarifying: "I am confused about…because…."
- Determining importance: "This is important because…."
- Visualizing: "The picture I see in my mind is…."

Two-Column Entries may include other text structures such as cause/effect, concept/definition, problem/solution, compare/contrast, and proposition/support.

3. Have students share their connections and thoughts with a partner.

Suggested Teacher Talk: *How does your personal connection support understanding?*

Comprehension Strategy: Predicting

Predicting is a strategy that helps readers set expectations for reading and decide what they think will happen. Strategic readers make predictions using information from the text and their experiences to anticipate what they will be reading. Their predictions are a *forecast* of an early sign of understanding. Predicting is based on a variety of strategies, including previewing, activating background knowledge, and asking questions (Duke & Pearson, 2002; Fisher et al., 2009). Readers use clues in the title, illustrations, and details within the text to make their predictions. Creating an *anticipatory set* is a way to generate readers' interest. Anticipation guides elicit analytical thinking to develop a *hypothesis* about the type, purpose, or scope of a text as the students make a prediction on a given statement (Herber & Nelson-Herber, 1987; Readence, Bean, & Baldwin, 1981, 2008; Wood, Lapp, Flood, & Taylor, 2008). Predictions can be used before reading as a frontloading strategy and as a downloading strategy during and after reading to confirm whether students' predictions were accurate, and students can adjust them as needed.

Key Vocabulary for Predicting

- Anticipatory Set: attention-getter/curiosity hook that generates interest by tapping into students' reactions to content information
- Forecast: an estimate or logical guess by the reader about what he or she thinks will happen or what he or she knows about a subject
- Hypothesis: a tentative explanation whose merit requires evaluation

Assessment for Predicting

Use the following behaviors as a guide as you assess students' abilities to predict. Do students exhibit these behaviors never, rarely, often, or always?

☐ Analyzes text traits and observes clues about topic or events

☐ Forecasts what a text will be about

☐ Confirms or modifies predictions

Teacher Talk: Statements, Questions, and Prompts for Predicting

The following are suggestions for teacher talk that encourages readers to think strategically as they employ the predicting strategy. Try using some of these statements, questions, and prompts with your students as you work through the techniques in the following section. They are aligned with Bloom's taxonomy and Webb's DOK levels.

Level of Thinking	Teacher Talk
Creating Extended Thinking	• What do you think the text is going to tell you about? What makes you think so? What evidence supports your prediction? How did you formulate your prediction?
Evaluating Strategic Thinking	• Justify your hypothesis. • How did the processes of predicting, modifying predictions, and confirming enhance your motivation before, during, and after reading? • What are the benefits of previewing keywords and phrases before reading? • Justify your thinking as you confirm or reassess your original response to the statements.
Analyzing Strategic Thinking	• What makes you think _____ is going to happen? • Which predictions were confirmed by the text? • Which predictions need to be adjusted or revised? • What are you reminded of when you reflect on the vocabulary words and phrases? • Do you agree or disagree with the statement presented?
Applying Skill/Concept	• Think about the text and imagine what is going on in the story. Which details or clues from the selection did you use to make your prediction?

Understanding Skill/Concept	• What do you predict the author will reveal next, based on the first paragraph or chapter?
	• What keywords supported you in making your prediction?
Remembering Recall	• What information do you expect to read in this selection based on the title?
	• Finish these thoughts: "I wonder if _____."; "I want to know _____."
	• Reflect on the keywords and phrases that you will see again in the text. What you think the text might be about?

Techniques for Predicting

Initial Sentences

Purpose: To examine opening sentences from content text and record, justify, or modify predictions

Multiple Intelligences: Visual/spatial, verbal/linguistic, interpersonal

Materials: Varied content texts

Procedure:

1. Have students explore and record the opening sentences from content text prior to reading the entire section, chapter, or complete text. By focusing on first lines (Allen, 2004), students analyze the initial sentences as foundation for their predictions.

2. After reading the initial sentences, students predict subsequent learning.

3. Encourage students to share their predictions and the clues used to make these forecasts within small groups. Capture individual or group predictions on chart paper or using a visual project device.

4. As students read the text resources through their coursework, they can revisit their predictions to discuss, confirm, or modify them.

Motivation/Engagement: *Intrapersonal.* Have the students explore the opening lines of various content area text from different disciplines. Record and collect the opening lines and generate predictions based on the initial sentences.

Suggested Teacher Talk: *How does using the Initial Sentences technique help to predict what might be discovered in the text? How did using the Initial Sentences technique provide clues to the author's pattern of organization?*

Passage/Concept Impressions

Purpose: To generate, assess, and justify evidence-based predictions

Multiple Intelligences: Verbal/linguistic, logical/mathematic, interpersonal

Materials: Fiction or nonfiction content-related text, chart paper or visual projection device

Procedure:

1. Select 7 to 10 keywords that relate to significant information from the text you are studying, and display the chain of words or phrases in the order in which they appeared in the text. For nonfiction texts, choose 10 or 12 vocabulary words and have students work with partners to create possible sentences using the presented words. Students may craft content-related sentences on varied topics. For fiction texts, words should reflect the following story elements: main characters, setting, problem, goal, events leading to the climax, and resolution (Ellery, 2009; McGinley & Denner, 1987).

Suggested Teacher Talk: *Try to imagine what is going on in the text based on the keywords presented.*

2. Have students work in teams to predict a story line (fiction) or events (nonfiction) using the words presented.

3. After students have had time to discuss their predictions, have teams create a story or passage using all the keywords. One student in the class can be the recorder and write the teams' creations on chart paper.

Suggested Teacher Talk: *Present your story creations to the entire class. Which details or clues did you use to make your prediction?*

4. After all the teams have shared their versions of the story or passage, have students compare and contrast their stories or passages.

Motivation/Engagement: *Visual/spatial.* Have students create a visual representation in a graphic organizer like a Venn diagram to compare and contrast their story or passage predictions to the original text.

Prediction Boxes

Purpose: To use authors' clues, illustrations, and key vocabulary to brainstorm, categorize, predict, and make personal connections prior to reading.

Multiple Intelligences: Visual/spatial, verbal/linguistic, interpersonal, intrapersonal

Materials: Multipurpose paper, print or online content text or both, chart paper or visual projection device; Optional: Prediction Boxes Grid reproducible (see Appendix)

Procedure:

1. Provide students with a plain 8½-by-11-inch piece of multipurpose paper to create their Prediction Boxes Grid (Caldwell & Ford, 2002). Students should fold the paper to yield six numbered prediction boxes. Figure 6.1 shows the six boxes and describes what goes in each box.

2. From the content text the students are preparing to read, select five to seven key vocabulary words or phrases for Box 1: Convergent Thinking. Display the list of words or phrases on a chart or visual projection device. Ask students to reflect on the initial words or phrases and write their predictions about what the text might be about in Box 1. Encourage students to share their prediction with a partner.

Suggested Teacher Talk: *Reflect on the words and phrases that you will see again in the text. In Box 1, write what you think the text might be about. What keywords supported you in making your prediction?*

3. Based on the previewed vocabulary, their generated predications, and partner discussions, guide students to make personal connections and capture their connections in Box 2: Making Connections.

Suggested Teacher Talk: *What are you reminded of when you reflect on the vocabulary words and phrases?*

4. Use an illustration or photograph that depicts the setting, topic, theme, or characters in the text. Have students use the picture to extend their predictions by reflecting on the visual image and enhancing or modifying their predictions in Box 3: Using Picture to Extend Prediction.

5. For Box 4: Revising Prediction, select an additional five to seven key vocabulary words or phrases. Display the list on a chart or visual projection device. Ask students to compare

FIGURE 6.1. Prediction Boxes Grid

Box 1: Convergent Thinking	Box 2: Making Connections	Box 3: Using Picture to Extend Prediction
Box 4: Revising Prediction	Box 5: Confirming Predictions	Box 6: Evaluating Performance

and contrast these additional words or phrases and with the terms in Box 1. Encourage students to identify and label some categories of information that surface from the words and phrases. Students should share their predictions with a partner.

Suggested Teacher Talk: *As you reflect on the words and phrases, modify or extend your prediction. What are some categories of information that help to organize the keywords and phrases?*

6. Read the text aloud or have students read independently. Remind students to focus on the keywords and phrases and to challenge or confirm their predictions.

7. After reading, guide students to confirm or challenge their predictions in Box 5: Confirming Predictions. Encourage students to share their predictions and confirmations with a partner after reading.

8. Have students reflect on the learning process in Box 6: Evaluating Performance.

Suggested Teacher Talk: *How did the processes of predicting, modifying predictions, and confirming enhance your motivation before, during, and after reading? What are the benefits of previewing keywords and phrases before reading?*

Anticipation/Reaction Guide

Purpose: To confirm or reassess predictions based on text evidence

Multiple Intelligences: Visual/spatial, verbal/linguistic, intrapersonal

Materials: Anticipation/Reaction Guide reproducible (see Appendix), content area text, student notebooks or journals, sticky notes or highlighters

Procedure:

1. Identify the main topic, major ideas, and concepts of a text prior to meeting with students.

2. Create six to eight statements that will challenge or support students' preexisting beliefs or that may reflect common misconceptions about the subject, topic, or concept. Write these on the Anticipation/Reaction Guide and provide students with print or electronic access. A balance of known information and new ideas will support students as they respond to the Anticipation/Reaction Guide statements (Buehl, 2009; Ellery, 2009; Herber, 1978; Santa, Havens, & Valdes, 2004). Record statements that students may concur with as well as statements that focus on possible misconceptions.

3. Have students read each statement and note by writing an *A* if they agree or writing a *D* if they disagree, so that students have a clear understanding of the process of predicting. Encourage students to generate evidence-based predictions, as some content area statements may be more challenging.

4. Students are encouraged to work independently as they reflect and respond to each statement on the Anticipation/Reaction Guide. Follow independent work with paired, small-group, or whole-group discussions.

5. Guide students to focus on confirming, reassessing, or modifying their predictions while reading. Students should use sticky notes or highlighters to note specific statements that align with the Anticipation/Reaction Guide statements.

Suggested Teacher Talk: *Do you agree or disagree with the statement presented? How did you formulate your prediction?*

6. Have students return to the statements after they have read the text and engage in a discussion on how the textual information supported, contradicted, or modified their first opinions. Students then record the support or evidence they found in the text.

Suggested Teacher Talk: *Justify your thinking as you confirm or reassess your original response to the statements. Which keywords or statements in the text support your ideas?*

Motivation/Engagement: *Interpersonal.* Using a similar content text source or another excerpt from the same text, assign each group of students a section of the text to create three to five statements for their own Anticipation/Reaction Guide. Using a chart or visual projection device, groups share their Anticipation/Reaction Guide statements and repeat the process for reading and confirming.

Comprehension Strategy: Inquiring and Inferring

Inquiring and Inferring are strategies that help readers to review content and relate what they have learned to what they already know through their ability to *hypothesize* about the text. Generating and asking questions supports students to identify issues and ideas in all content areas, construct meaning prior to reading, enhance understanding, discover new information, clarify, and solve problems. Making an inquiry before reading allows readers to set purposes for reading and helps them to determine what they want to learn while reading. *Shared inquiry* (Wheelock, 1999) encourages readers to explore together as they interact with the text.

Inferring is a powerful strategy that permits readers to merge their background knowledge, ask questions, make judgments from textual clues, and *extrapolate* meaning when it is not directly stated by the author. When learners infer, they go beyond the exterior details to create unique understandings of the text and extend beyond literal understanding (Keene & Zimmermann, 2007; Zwiers, 2010). When learners gather ideas and *draw conclusions*, they are able to choose the most likely explanation from the evidence in the text. They infer by reasoning from known facts or evidence that seem to require that a specific conclusion be reached to form *implied meaning*. "Inferring is the bedrock of comprehension, not only in reading . . . inferring is about reading faces, reading body language, reading expressions, and reading tone, as well as reading text" (Harvey & Goudvis, 2000, p. 105). When learners are inferring the content, as well as inferring in their everyday lives, they use *implicit* information to give a logical guess or read between the lines: "Individuals constantly make inferences as they engage in conversations with their friends, watch movies, or participate in other aspects of life" (Nokes, 2008, p. 541).

Key Vocabulary for Inquiring and Inferring

- Draw Conclusions: to combine several pieces of information to infer the author's point of view

- Extrapolate: to draw and expand from what is known

- Hypothesize: to form a tentative assumption that needs evaluation

- Implicit: understood or stated indirectly

- Implied Meaning: an idea that is not stated outright but is hinted

- Shared Inquiry: with other readers, posing questions that do not have a preconceived answer

Assessment for Inquiring and Inferring

Use the following behaviors as a guide as you assess students' abilities to inquire and infer. Do students exhibit these behaviors never, rarely, often, or always?

☐ Establishes a purpose for reading by asking questions

☐ Generates questions to discover new information prior to reading

☐ Merges background knowledge and textual clues to construct interpretations of text

Teacher Talk: Statements, Questions, and Prompts for Inquiring and Inferring

The following are suggestions for teacher talk that encourages readers to think strategically as they employ the inquiring and inferring strategy. Try using some of these statements, questions, and prompts with your students as you work through the techniques in the following section. They are aligned with Bloom's taxonomy and Webb's DOK levels.

Level of Thinking	Teacher Talk
Creating Extended Thinking	• Reflect on how asking questions helps the reader. How does forming a question about the text help you comprehend it? • What is the author trying to tell us with the text supports and features? • Create the story that you think is happening between the lines. What evidence does the author provide to support…?
Evaluating Strategic Thinking	• Try to think of a question that will support comprehension of the text. • What do you understand now because of your questions? • How does self-questioning support understanding?

	• How do you combine the clues in the paragraph with what you already know to draw a conclusion?
	• What reasoning helped you draw your conclusion?
Analyzing Strategic Thinking	• What clues does the genre style provide for gaining insight prior to reading? What are some unanswered questions?
	• What facts can you derive based on the following clues…?
	• What does the author want you to realize from this section?
	• What would happen if…? Why do you think that would happen?
Applying Skill/Concept	• What questions do you hope this text will answer?
	• Before you start reading, ask three questions about the topic that you would like the text to answer.
	• What is the story beneath the story?
	• What facts can you derive based on the following clues? Make a prediction.
Understanding Skill/Concept	• What are clues to help answer your inquiries?
	• What clues did the author give that led to your conclusion?
	• What details or evidence supports your conclusion?
Remembering Recall	• Finish this thought: "I wonder…."
	• What is the main conclusion from…?"
	• Finish this thought: "This statement means…."

Techniques for Inquiring and Inferring

Reflect on Questions

Purpose: To reflect on types of questions to establish a purpose for reading

Multiple Intelligences: Visual/spatial, verbal/linguistic, interpersonal, interpersonal

Materials: Questioning Matrix, text

Procedure:

1. Teacher and students read a targeted passage of content text silently. When selecting the text, take into account its level of difficulty and vary the text to align it with student abilities. The selected passages may be one sentence or several paragraphs in length.

2. Revisit or explore the characteristics of varied levels of questions and sample questions (see Text Inquiry technique in this Inquiring and Inferring strategy section). Vary the questioning process by using an adaptation of the ReQuest (Kane, 2007; Manzo, 1969).

Students ask the teacher comprehension questions relating to the content passage. Focus on the varied levels of questions (Goatley & Raphael, 1992) by providing access to Figure 6.2, Questioning Matrix. Model the process of generating questions by crafting a question from the text passage and justifying the type of question as well as your own thought process.

Suggested Teacher Talk: *Reflect on your thinking as you generated questions. Justify your choice of question starters (question words) to align with the levels of questions.*

3. Reverse roles so that the teacher asks the students varied levels of comprehension questions relating to the next section or passage in the text. Continue this process with subsequent sentences or passages.

4. Prior to completing the entire segment of content text, encourage the students to establish a defined purpose for reading by making a prediction about the remainder of the text.

Suggested Teacher Talk: *How does self-questioning help you establish a purpose for reading the rest of the content passage?*

5. Facilitate a postreading discussion comparing and contrasting the varied levels of questions and encouraging the use of higher order thinking and questioning.

Suggested Teacher Talk: *Describe the relationship between literal, interpretive, and evaluative questions and your thinking process as you generated comprehension questions.*

Motivation/Engagement: *Logical/mathematical.* Present examples of open questions (Small, 2010) like those in the following list, or a broader question that encourages choice and varied levels of responses. Provide students with answers to the content question and have the students respond with the questions.

- *The answer is _____. What might the question be?* (The answer is c^2. What might the question be?)

FIGURE 6.2. Questioning Matrix

Levels of Questioning	Question–Answer Relationships	Descriptors
Literal	Right There	Answer is targeted in the text (*Where? How many? What?*)
Interpretive	Think & Search	Answer is in the text, but in more than one location (*What are the reasons...? Identify three causes for...?*)
Evaluative	Author and You	Reader makes connections to text (*The author suggests.... The text purposes to....*
Critical	On My Own	Reader makes personal connections based on central themes, ideas, and emotions presented in the text (*My opinion is.... My experience leads me to believe....*)

Note. Adapted from Wood, Lapp, Flood, & Taylor, 2008.

- *How are _____ and _____ alike? How are they different?* (How are *immigration* and *relocation* alike? How are they different?)

- *Initiate a one-minute conversation with your partner using the concepts of _____, _____, and _____.* (Initiate a one-minute conversation with your partner using the concepts of *mean, median,* and *mode*).

Authentic Questions (3Rs)

Purpose: To record, react, and reflect on real, authentic questions that surface during reading to move toward a deeper understanding of content text

Comprehension: Inquiring and Inferring

Multiple Intelligences: Visual/spatial, verbal/linguistic, interpersonal

Materials: Student notebooks or journals, content text

Procedure:

1. Students can create their own 3R Question Logs (Ellery, 2009) by folding a piece of multipurpose paper lengthwise to make three columns. Label each column: *1R* for recording questions; *2R* for reactions; and *3R* for reflections. Students use their 3R Question Logs to capture key questions.

2. *Record*: Discuss and model types of authentic questions (Santa et al., 2004) that surface as you read (e.g., challenging concepts, historical events, steps or procedures, literary elements). Record example student-generated questions and facilitate a class discussion of possible answers to some of the questions.

Suggested Teacher Talk: *As you are reading, record any questions that surface. Which questions does the author address within the text?*

3. *Reactions*: As they continue to read, encourage students to note their reactions in the 2R column.

Suggested Teacher Talk: *What did you wonder about while reading the text? What are some unanswered questions?*

4. *Reflections*: In the 3R column, students record reflections and connections after reading.

Motivation/Engagement: *Intrapersonal.* Encourage students to reflect on the process of generating authentic questions while reading. They can record their thoughts in the final (3R) column of their question log.

Suggested Teacher Talk: *How does self-questioning support understanding?*

Text Inquiry

Purpose: To understand and apply varied types of questions and stimulate thinking about the reader's role in answering questions

Multiple Intelligences: Visual/spatial, verbal/linguistic, logical/mathematical, interpersonal

Materials: Questioning Matrix (see Figure 6.2 in the Reflect on Questions technique in this chapter), content text, multipurpose paper, student notebooks or journals

Procedure:

1. Using the Questioning Matrix support students to explore the characteristics of varied levels of questions and sample questions. Focus student discussions to recognize that the levels of questions presented in Question–Answer Relationships (Raphael, 1986; Raphael, Highfield, & Au, 2006) and Learning From Text Guides (Wood, Lapp, Flood, & Taylor, 2008) can be aligned based on the levels of thinking needed to derive answers.

2. Using a familiar content passage, model crafting varied levels of questions and chart sample questions as a visual support.

3. Students will work in pairs or small groups to practice answering the different types of questions, which should be crafted by the teacher in advance. Encourage teams to craft questions representing the varied levels of questions and justify their responses in student notebooks or journals.

Suggested Teacher Talk: *How does the level of questions guide your thinking as you answer questions?*

4. Have students share their questions, levels, and possible answers with the whole group. Discuss any challenging areas and reread to confirm accuracy of answers.

Motivation/Engagement: *Intrapersonal.* Using sample content assessment questions and text questions, students use the characteristics presented in the Questioning Matrix to determine levels of questions.

Suggested Teacher Talk: *Which levels of questioning are most often noted in class assessment? Which levels are more frequently used in the content text questioning? How does understanding how to craft varied levels of questions support in effectively responding to questions?*

Save the Last Word

Purpose: To make personal connections to information in the text, construct interpretations, and compare the interpretations with others

Multiple Intelligences: Visual/spatial, verbal/linguistic, bodily/kinesthetic, interpersonal

Materials: Text, note cards

Procedure:

1. Choose a text that may elicit differing opinions or multiple interpretations. As students read the passage, have them select five statements that they find interesting or would like to comment on—statements they agree or disagree with or that contradict something they thought they knew.

2. Students write one statement on the front of each of the five index cards. On the back of each card, they write the comment they want to share with the group about that statement.

3. Place students in small groups. When students meet in their group, they select one person to go first. That person reads the statement from the front of one of his or her cards, but is not allowed to comment. All other students, in turn, respond to the statement, make comments, share what they think the quote or statement means, and agree or disagree.

4. When the discussion eventually moves around to the student who wrote the statement, that student flips over their index card and has *the last word* as he or she explain why it was selected. This student has an opportunity to adjust his or her comments and reflect on ideas before expressing them to the group.

5. The sharing process is repeated until everyone in the group has had *the last word*. This technique can be used as an after-reading activity in all subjects for almost any topic and offers reluctant speakers an opportunity to safely share their ideas and discover common elements.

Ripple Effect

Purpose: To generate questions and stimulate dialogues based on the questions

Multiple Intelligences: Visual/spatial, verbal/linguistic, bodily/kinesthetic, interpersonal, naturalistic/environmental

Materials: Text; Optional: a picture of a still lake or pond

Comprehension: Inquiring and Inferring

Procedure:

1. Select a text, theme, or concept to introduce to the class.

2. Have the students visualize what happens when you throw a pebble into a still lake. There is a splash, and you may never hear the pebble hit the water. You will notice concentric circles rippling out from the entry point. Students may even describe other effects when the pebble enters the water (e.g., scare a fish, hit another rock, frighten someone near the pond). By throwing the pebble into the water, you have caused change through the ripple effect.

3. Connect this visualization to what happens in your head as you think about a story or idea. The pebble can represent a question that you form and toss out into the sea of unknown. A ripple of thoughts or a wave of thinking begins to spread and expand from the point of origin.

4. During a read-aloud, model for students when a thought or question occurs in your mind; stop and toss the pebble into the water. Share the question and let the "wave of thinking" ripple into the conversation about the text. Depending on how deep the concept, the waves can lead to further research and more reading. Students work independently or in small groups to initiate the ripple effect by posing a question aloud for others to respond to and discuss.

Motivation/Engagement: *Logical/mathematical*. It is important to teach students to ask inferential and applied-level questions. These higher level questions help students to think more critically. They will enjoy creating questions that cover the reading, along with the accompanying answer document.

Comprehension Strategy: Determining Importance

Determining importance enables learners to distinguish the most important information that highlights the *essential* ideas, concepts, or theme of a text. Readers determine what is important based on the purpose of reading and their ability to evaluate what are the most critical *details* to support the overall meaning. Strategic readers can determine the difference between an important detail and an interesting fact that supports the *main idea*: "Readers cannot store all the information presented in a text in their minds. *Sifting* [emphasis added] through information to determine the most important points ensures that working memory is not overloaded and continues to process information" (Fisher et al., 2009, p. 51). Before and after reading, *sensory language* supports readers to form appropriate mental images, providing a springboard for recall of descriptive details within the text. Determining importance allows reading to be an active process by stimulating the mental interchange of new ideas and experiences and creating sensory images. Forming these images during reading seems to increase the amount readers understand and recall for important details (Irwin, 1991; Johnston, Barnes, & Desrochers, 2008; Sprenger, 2005). Determining importance allows learners to process the value of information in fiction and nonfiction text in all disciplines by prioritizing the content for deeper understanding.

Key Vocabulary for Determining Importance

- Details: specific ideas and facts that are critical to the topic or content

- Essential: fundamental to bringing meaning

- Main Idea: the most important fact, concept, or idea of the text

- Sensory Language: words that convey the connections between the ideas and the five senses

- Sifting: evaluating and sorting details to find those that are important

Assessment for Determining Importance

Use the following behaviors as a guide as you assess students' abilities to determine importance. Do students exhibit these behaviors never, rarely, often, or always?

☐ Determines essential information (key idea, theme, or concept)

☐ Uses supporting details from the text to clearly explain why information is important

☐ Uses senses to attend to text details

Teacher Talk: Statements, Questions, and Prompts for Determining Importance

The following are suggestions for teacher talk that encourages readers to think strategically as they employ the determining importance strategy. Try using some of these statements, questions, and prompts with your students as you work through the techniques in the following section. They are aligned with Bloom's taxonomy and Webb's DOK levels.

Level of Thinking	Teacher Talk
Creating Extended Thinking	• Think about the facts and create questions you have about the information presented. • Generate evidence that the author used to support his or her case. • What sensory details did the author use to help you create a picture of the story or information in your mind?
Evaluating Strategic Thinking	• What do you think the author is trying to tell you? • Which facts are important or essential to the text? Why? • Justify why you chose to highlight this part: "I chose to highlight this part because…."
Analyzing Strategic Thinking	• How did you know these details were more important than other details? • Describe the difference between what you need to know and what is just interesting.
Applying Skill/Concept	• What is essential? • Which facts are important or essential to the text? • What is the author's message? • Explain what the author offers as a theme or opinion.
Understanding Skill/Concept	• What does the author offer as a theme or opinion? • Notice that the cue words are followed by important information. What are the most important in this reading?

| Remembering | • Use the margin to make notes. Highlight only necessary words and phrases. |
| Recall | |

- Answer this question: "What should I remember?"
- Look carefully at the first and last line of each paragraph.
- Tell me about some of the important ideas that struck you.

Techniques for Determining Importance

Main Idea Wheel

Purpose: To identify the main ideas and important details in challenging content text

Multiple Intelligences: Visual/spatial, verbal/linguistic, interpersonal

Materials: Main Idea Wheel reproducible (see Appendix), text

Procedure:

1. Begin by modeling using a whiteboard or visual projection device. Choose a familiar text and read an excerpt aloud. Have students determine the main idea and record it in the center of the wheel. Students decide which details are most important or essential to developing the main idea. Model the process for recording the main idea and details on the main idea wheel.

2. Have students work with partners to create a Main Idea Wheel for a novel or nonfiction content text you are reading in class. Students will record the identified main idea and details on their own wheels. This makes a guide for small- or whole-group discussion.

Motivation/Engagement: *Bodily/kinesthetic.* Create a large Main Idea Wheel on chart paper or in an electronic format. Choose a content text and as a group determine the main idea. Divide students into groups with each being assigned a different section or chapter of text to determine the essential details. One member of each group will bring their piece of the Main Idea Wheel to a designated display area in the classroom. As each group adds their piece, a class Main Idea Wheel is created as a visual of the main idea and details in the text.

Narrative and Nonfiction Pyramids

Purpose: To organize key elements from content text

Multiple Intelligences: Visual/spatial, verbal/linguistic, logical/mathematical

Materials: Narrative Pyramid reproducible (see Appendix), Nonfiction Pyramid reproducible (see Appendix), text, paper

Procedure:

1. Have students determine which pyramid they will be using based on either narrative or nonfiction text. If it is a narrative text, have them construct an eight-line narrative pyramid of words (Ellery, 2009; Schwartz & Bone, 1995) before using the Narrative Pyramid reproducible. If the text is nonfiction, they can use the Nonfiction Pyramid reproducible to process the information.

Suggested Teacher Talk: *Think of all the parts in the text and put them together as if you were to tell another person the "story" or key points of the text.*

2. The first line of the narrative will contain the character's name in a single word. For nonfiction, this will be one major idea.

3. For the second line, have students use two words to describe that character. For nonfiction, this will be two supporting details.

4. For the third line, students write three words to portray the setting, or they can add three different locations. For nonfiction, this will be a major idea, or a geographical location if applicable.

5. For the fourth line, ask students to explain the problem using four descriptive words or four specific conflicts occurring in the text. For nonfiction, if a conflict or problem isn't applicable, students write four words describing another supporting detail.

6. For lines five, six, and seven, students describe three different events that occurred and use the corresponding number of words for their lines. For nonfiction, if three different events don't apply, these lines can include author's purpose and vocabulary words.

7. For the eighth line, the student selects eight words to express the solution to the problem or conflict.

8. Have students use their pyramids to give an oral summary of the text.

Suggested Teacher Talk: *Using your pyramid, describe the detail in the content.*

Highlighting the Highs

Purpose: To determine important information and ideas in text for understanding, discussion, or writing

Multiple Intelligences: Verbal/linguistic, interpersonal, intrapersonal

Materials: Varied content texts, highlighters or small sticky notes

Procedure:

1. Students should skim or preview the passage, focusing on text structure (e.g., boldfaced headings, subheadings, key vocabulary) and the author's purpose.

Suggested Teacher Talk: *What message is the author communicating in the passage?*

Comprehension: Determining Importance

2. Model the process for highlighting important information. Use a think-aloud to model the following tips for effective highlighting:

- Be selective in highlighting; focus on key ideas, new vocabulary, and ideas that you find surprising.

- Highlight keywords and phrases rather than whole sentences.

- Use sticky notes or marginal notes to jot down your thoughts, questions, and concerns while reading.

- Read one or two paragraphs at a time and then highlight.

- You are probably highlighting too much information if your page appears fluorescent.

3. Encourage students to share their highlighted information and work with a partner to read, discuss, and highlight the highs in the next section of text.

Suggested Teacher Talk: *Justify your reasoning for selecting your highlighted information.*

Motivation/Engagement: *Visual/spatial.* With students in small groups, assign each group a section of text to read, discuss, and highlight the highs. Student groups collaborate to compare and justify their highlighted information as they prepare to "teach" the key ideas from their assigned passage to the whole class. Groups can use picture notes, webbing, or two-column note-taking to create a visual representation as they share their section with the class.

Suggested Teacher Talk: *Ask yourself, "How can I structure this information to make it my own?"*

Comprehension Strategy: Summarizing and Synthesizing

Summarizing is a strategy that enables the reader to identify and organize essential information by putting together key elements of what they are reading. Students continually organize these *key elements* throughout their reading of a text while filtering out less significant details. Research suggests instruction on summarizing can improve students' overall comprehension of text content (Duke & Pearson, 2002). Summarizing includes selecting important information, making *generalizations*, and succinctly reducing the passage into a compilation of facts. Text guides can support the readers to deconstruct the main ideas to form a summary (Montelongo, 2008).

Synthesizing merges the summary of new information with prior background knowledge to create an original idea. Strategic readers stop periodically while reading to digest what they have read, allowing them to make judgments that promote higher order, *elaborative thinking.* This thinking process combines the results of developing thoughts into a conclusion to interpret or evaluate, and adds information to the summary (Fisher et al., 2009). The ability to synthesize when reading integrates all of the comprehension strategies described previously in this chapter—which itself, actually, is synthesizing.

Key Vocabulary for Summarizing and Synthesizing

- Elaborative Thinking: to expand from detail; concurs in conjunction with analysis of the information

- Generalizations: broad understandings reached by applying inductive reasoning

- Key Elements: brief and related ideas, events, details, structural clues, or other information that supports the reader in bringing meaning to the text

Assessment for Summarizing and Synthesizing

Use the following behaviors as a guide as you assess students' abilities to summarize and synthesize. Do students exhibit these behaviors never, rarely, often, or always?

- ☐ Identifies and organizes essential information

- ☐ Monitors and evaluates text for meaning

- ☐ Combines information and forms new thoughts based on that information

Teacher Talk: Statements, Questions, and Prompts for Summarizing and Synthesizing

The following are suggestions for teacher talk that encourages readers to think strategically as they employ the summarizing and synthesizing strategy. Try using some of these statements, questions, and prompts with your students as you work through the techniques in the following section. They are aligned with Bloom's taxonomy and Webb's DOK levels.

Level of Thinking	Teacher Talk
Creating Extended Thinking	• What new ideas or information do you have after reading this text? • Create a new idea based on parts form this information. • Propose an alternative to the situation.
Evaluating Strategic Thinking	• How can you use key ideas to condense the information in this story? • How could you test your theory? • What do you understand now that you did not understand before? • How has your thinking changed since reading that part of the text?

Analyzing Strategic Thinking	• How can you describe your overall understanding of the story in a few sentences?
	• Which details are most and least significant to the overall meaning?
	• Which words helped you describe the gist of the story?
Applying Skill/Concept	• Think of all the parts in the story and put them together as if you were going to tell another person about the story. How could you summarize or say this using only a few sentences?
Understanding Skill/Concept	• Complete this statement: "The text is mainly about...."
	• What was the focus of the reading selection?
	• What is the gist of the story?
Remembering Recall	• What clues are within the text?

Techniques for Summarizing and Synthesizing

Diverge/Converge

Comprehension: Summarizing and Synthesizing

Purpose: To organize, capture key concepts, and summarize challenging content text

Multiple Intelligences: Visual/spatial, verbal/linguistic, bodily/kinesthetic

Materials: Note cards for each student, content text passages, chart paper or visual projection device, available technology resources; Optional: Get to the Point reproducible (see Appendix), Main Idea Wheel (see Appendix)

Procedure:

1. Group students into groups for the Diverge part of this technique. Assign each group a section of content text.

2. Model and review various summarizing tools, such as using the Get to the Point reproducible (see Appendix), Main Idea Wheel (see Main Idea Wheel technique in the previous Determining Importance strategy section), graphic organizers, or technology tools (e.g., SMART Board or Promethean interactive whiteboard)

3. Divergent thinking involves pulling a topic apart to explore its various components. To illustrate this process, each group is responsible for determining key information and ideas from their section of text and using a visual representation to "teach-back" in a whole-group setting. Each visual representation must include a written summary statement.

4. Post a large piece of chart paper or use a visual projection device to display the groups' visual representations. In the center of the chart, present the title of the chapter or article from which the groups' text sections were drawn.

5. To reassemble, or converge, the different ideas (convergent thinking) each group will present a 3–5 minute teach-back. Encourage students to question, discuss, and note key ideas from each group presentation.

Suggested Teacher Talk: *How did the groups' visual representations support you in creating a summary statement?*

6. As each group presents, they add their visual display around the chapter or article title.

7. Facilitate a whole-group debrief of the summarizing process.

Motivation/Engagement: *Logical/mathematical.* Encourage students to create a one-sentence summary statement capturing the gist, or key ideas, presented in the chapter or article by using all the groups' visual representations and summary statements. Share summary statements in pairs, small groups, or as a whole group.

Somebody Wanted But So

Purpose: To use a tool for summarizing information and ideas, making connections, and remembering important information

> **Comprehension:
> Summarizing
> and Synthesizing**

Multiple Intelligences: Visual/spatial, verbal/linguistic, intrapersonal

Materials: Fiction or nonfiction narrative text, Somebody Wanted But So (SWBS) organizer

Procedure:

1. Model using Somebody Wanted But So (Ellery, 2009; Schmidt & Buckley, 1990) to retell a life event or a movie. Write the SWBS framework on the board or overhead in a four-column chart. Students will identify the *Somebody* as the main character or historical figure, as you record it on the chart.

2. Explain that *Wanted* represents the plot or motivation that is occurring to the *Somebody*. Record the students' responses in the *Wanted* column.

3. Explain that *But* stands for the conflict or challenge the *Somebody* faces. Record students' responses on the chart.

4. Share that *So* represents the outcome or resolution. Record student responses in the *So* column.

5. Read aloud the summary statement that the SWBS framework creates.

6. Have students use the SWBS chart to summarize a narrative text that they all have read. Have them share as you record responses in the chart on the board.

7. Explain how students can use this SWBS framework to help them summarize any narrative text. If they are using this technique with a longer novel, they can write a SWBS for each chapter. It also helps students identify main ideas and details, recognize cause-and-effect relationships, make generalizations, and analyze points of view.

Variations: Nonfiction Frameworks

Something happens *Then* this occurs *Which* results in

A _____ is a kind of _____ that _____.

Get to the Point

Comprehension:
Summarizing
and Synthesizing

Purpose: To combine information and form new thoughts, going from divergent to convergent thinking

Multiple Intelligences: Visual/spatial, verbal/linguistic, interpersonal, intrapersonal

Materials: Get to the Point reproducible (see Appendix), text

Procedure:

1. Model on visual projection device or chalkboard the Get to the Point framework. Read together a portion of a passage from the text and have students share their thoughts. Record these thoughts in the outside circle.

2. Read another portion of the passage and then stop. Have students formulate new thoughts and record them in the next circle.

3. Read a final portion, or reread the passage if it is especially challenging. Have students summarize or synthesize all thoughts on this framework into one sentence and record it in the center circle.

4. Students work with a partner and a new text or passage. After reading half of the passage, they will record their first thinking in the outside circle.

5. Partners then finish reading the passage and record their new thoughts in the next circle. Students then reread, reflect, and discuss how they can converge all ideas into one main point.

6. Have students share their final thoughts and how the concept of Get to the Point helped them synthesize the main idea.

Appendix

Appendix reproducibles are listed in the order in which they are referred to in the text. The technique(s) with which the reproducible is used is in parentheses following the reproducible title.

Comprehension: Frontloading and Downloading

ROLL-READ-RECORD GRAPHING CHART

Roll-Read-Record (3Rs)

Name:_____ Date: _____

Title: _____

1	2	3	4	5	6

Roll-Read-Record (3Rs)

Name:_____ Date: _____

Title: _____

1	2	3	4	5	6

Roll-Read-Record (3Rs)

Name:_____ Date: _____

Title: _____

1	2	3	4	5	6

DISSECT

Name:_____ Date:_____

Discover the context	Isolate the prefix	Separate the suffix	Say the stem	Examine the stem	Check with someone	Try another resource

Word definition: _____

COMMON CONTENT AREA ROOTS AND AFFIXES

Common Root, Prefix or Suffix	Meaning	Science	Social Studies	Mathematics
-able	capable or worthy of	invisible, predictable	adaptable, acceptable, remarkable	divisible
-ation	forms nouns from verbs	creation, information, determination	civilization, automation, speculation	interpretation, evaluation
de	down, from	detach, deodorize, decompose	deploy, destruction, depression	descend, decrease
demo	people	epidemic	democracy, demographic	
dia	through, between, across		diagram, dialect, dialogue	diameter, diagonal, diagram
dict	to say	predict, contradict	dictate, edict	
di-, dys-, dif-	not, negative	disperse, disconnect	differ, dysfunction	difference
equi	equal	equilibrium, equator	equinox, equitable	equation, equidistant, equilateral, equal
ex-	former, completely	external	exit, exalt, exclude	expanded
exter, extra	outside of	external, extract, extrasensory	extradite, extrinsic, extreme	exterior
frag, fract	break	fracture, fragment	fraction	fraction
flux, flu	flow	fluctuate	influence, influx	reflux, confluence
graph, gram	to write	polygraph, graphite, electrocardiogram	biography, telegram, historiography	graph, graphic
gress	to walk	progress	transgress, digress	
hyper	over, above	hypersensitive, hyperventilate, hyperkinetic, hypersonic	hyperlink, hypertext	hyperbole
inter-	between	intermittent	international	intercept
log, logo, loc	word, speak	logic	monologue, dialogue, eulogy	logarithm
mal	bad, badly	malaria, malfunction, malformation	malice, malady, malcontent	
-ity, -ty	state of, quality of	electricity, peculiarity, certainty	subtlety, cruelty, frailty, loyalty, royalty	similarity, technicality
meta	beyond, change	metamorphosis, metabolism	metacognitive, metahistorical	
meter	measure	micrometer, altimeter, thermometer, multimeter		perimeter, metrics, geometry, kilometer
multi	many	multimedia	multitude, multipartite, multinational	multiplication
non-	not	nonabrasive, nonfat, nonferrous, nonskid, nonmetallic	nonfiction, nonprofit, nonresident, nonviolence	noncollinear, noncoplanar, nonessential
pan	all, whole	pandemic, panacea, panorama	pandemonium, panoply, pan-American	
para	beside	paramedic, parachute	paraphrase, compare	parabola, parallel
pend	to hang	pendulum	append, depend, impend	
peri	around	periscope, periodontal		perimeter
poly	many	polymorphous	polytheist, polygamy	polygon, polynomial
re-	again, back	remake, return	rerun, rewrite	rearrange, rebuild, recall
scrib, script	to write	describe, prescribe	subscribe	describe
sect, sec	cut	dissect	section	intersect
sub-	under	subsoil, substandard, subhuman	submarine, subway, subtitles	subset
struct	build	structure	instruct	construct
-tract	to pull, drag, draw	attract, extract	contract, retract	protract, subtract
-vert	to turn	convert, invert	divert, revert, extravert	vertical, invert

WORD ROOT TREE

Word Root Tree Template

Word Root Tree Template

Word Root Tree Template

Word Root Tree Template

SLOW TO FLOW GUIDE

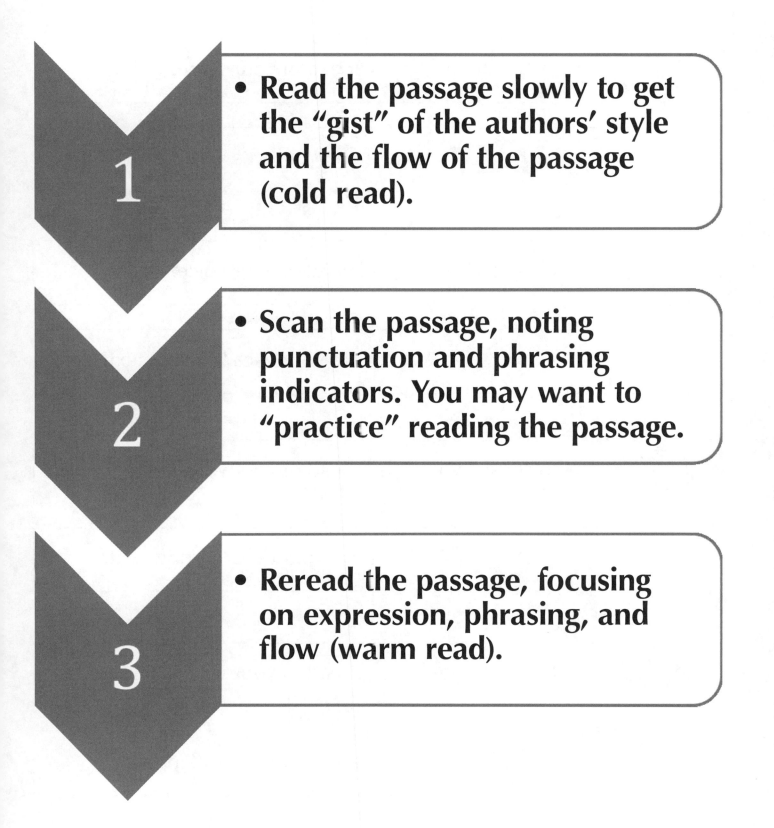

1
- Read the passage slowly to get the "gist" of the authors' style and the flow of the passage (cold read).

2
- Scan the passage, noting punctuation and phrasing indicators. You may want to "practice" reading the passage.

3
- Reread the passage, focusing on expression, phrasing, and flow (warm read).

PHRASE TALK STRIPS

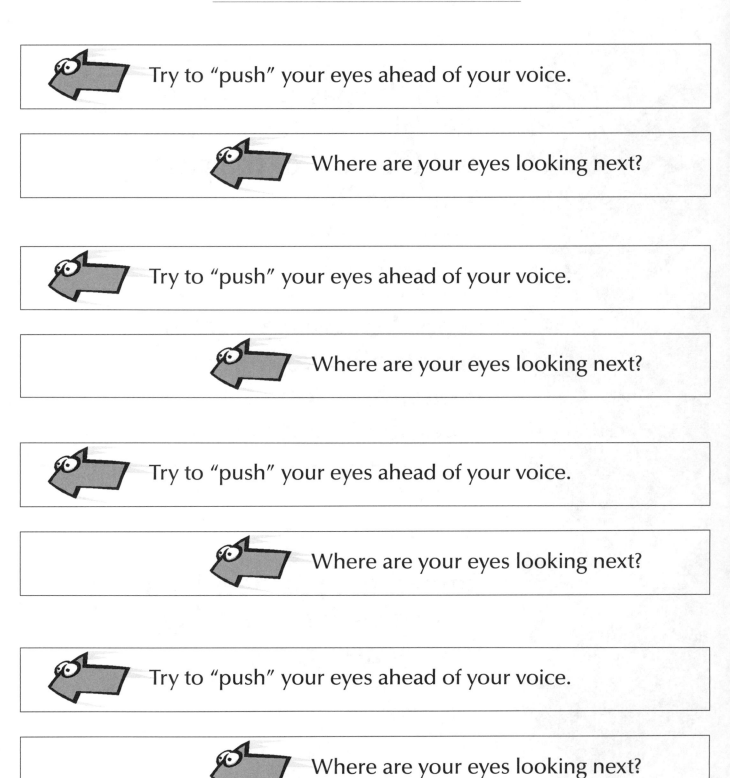

Try to "push" your eyes ahead of your voice.

Where are your eyes looking next?

Try to "push" your eyes ahead of your voice.

Where are your eyes looking next?

Try to "push" your eyes ahead of your voice.

Where are your eyes looking next?

Try to "push" your eyes ahead of your voice.

Where are your eyes looking next?

PARTNER READING BOOKMARK

Before:

_____ Reads title/heading and makes predictions

_____ Skims and scans section to preview

During:

_____ Reads a passage

_____ Makes meaningful phrases with attention to expression

_____ Reads smoothly

_____ Paces with a conversational flow

After:

_____ Asks a question about the information

_____ Summarizes a page

_____ Points out key vocabulary and concepts

_____ Predicts what will happen next

Sustaining Strategic Readers: Techniques for Supporting Content Literacy in Grades 6–12 by Valerie Ellery and Jennifer L. Rosenboom.
© 2011 International Reading Association. May be copied for classroom use.

EXPRESSION CARDS

exhausted

confused

ecstatic

guilty

suspicious

angry

hysterical

frustrated

sad

confident

embarrassed

happy

mischievous

disgusted

frightened

METHODS FOR DETERMINING DEVELOPMENTAL READING LEVELS

Method	Range of Levels and Frequency	Description & Grouping	Components and Measured Indicators
Guided Reading (Grades K–12) Fountas and Pinnell (2001)	A–Z Ongoing (quarterly)	1–1 Evaluation; student reads aloud and teacher maintains reading record of performance; student retells	Comprehension Accuracy
Developmental Reading Assessment 2 (DRA) (Grade 4–8) Beaver (2003)	A, 1–44 Ongoing (2–3 times a year)	1–1 Evaluation; student reads aloud and teacher maintains reading record of performance; student retells	Comprehension Accuracy Fluency (WPM) Combines total score using data from Oral Reading Fluency and Comprehension sections for a total continuum
Lexile	200– 1700 + (yearly)	Standardized reading inventory Proprietary tests	Comprehension
Individual Reading Inventories (IRIs)	Graded word lists and passages with number of words ranging from 354 to 1,224 (quarterly)	Individualized	Comprehension Accuracy Fluency (WPM)
Fry Readability Graph	Ongoing	Randomly selects three 100-word passages; plots the average number of syllables and the average number of sentences per 100 words on the graph	Accuracy
Flesh-Kincaid Readability Formula (Microsoft Word)	Ongoing	Microsoft Word has a built-in grade reader; randomly select 100 words of a text and the program will determine the grade level according to the word count and syllables	Accuracy

PASS THE BOOK REFLECTION GUIDE

Title of Book	Author(s)	Reactions

ACTIVE ANALOGIES

Types of Analogies:	Examples
Synonym Relationship	average:mean
Classification Relationship	frog:amphibian
Cause-and-Effect Relationship	5:25
Part-to-Whole Relationship	poem:stanza
Function Relationship	knife:cut
Purpose Relations	ruler:line

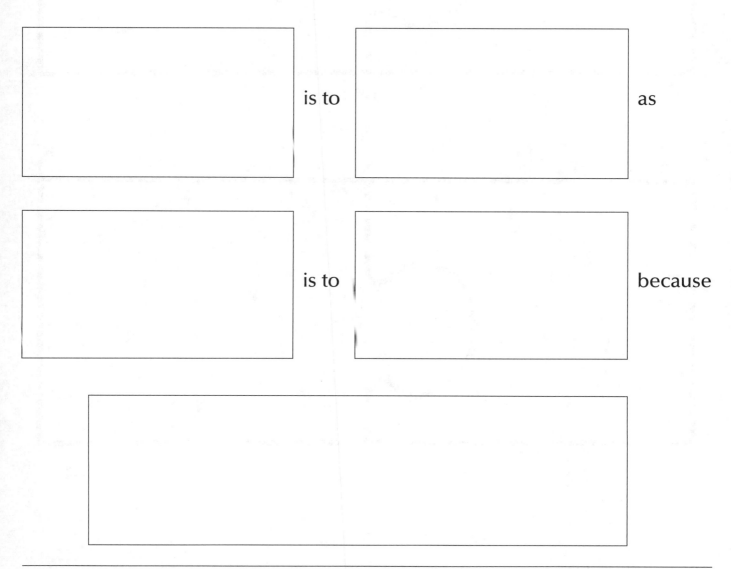

is to ___ as

is to ___ because

REFLECTION CONNECTION PUZZLE PIECE

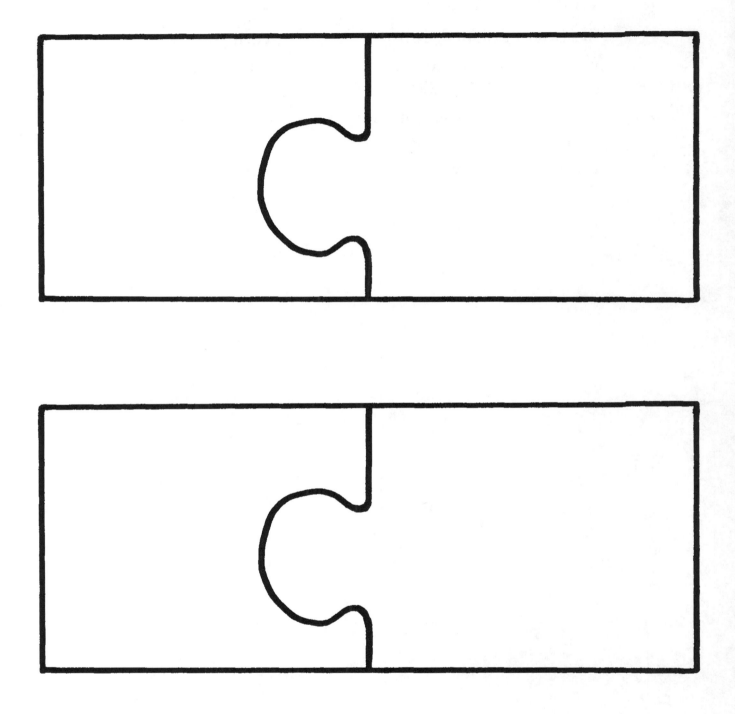

WORD-NET WHEEL

Title: _____

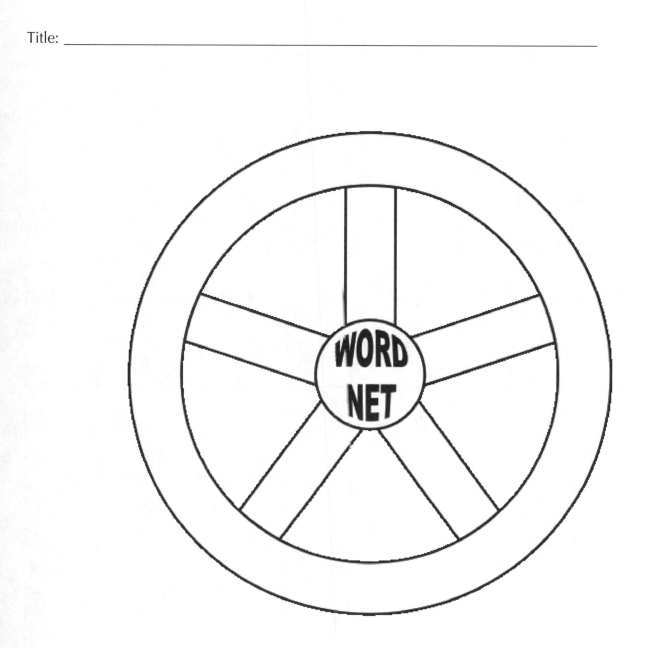

SEMANTIC FEATURE ANALYSIS MATRIX

Name _____

Date _____

Text _____

	Characteristics, Properties, Features, Elements						
(Check one) ☐ Examples ☐ Categories ☐ Vocabulary words ☐ Phrases ☐ Concepts							

Adapted from Baldwin et al., 1981

WORD RELATIONSHIPS

Unique Attributes

Similar Attributes

Unique Attributes

Adapted from Hyerle, 2004

Sustaining Strategic Readers: Techniques for Supporting Content Literacy in Grades 6–12 by Valerie Ellery and Jennifer L. Rosenboom.
© 2011 International Reading Association. May be copied for classroom use.

CHALLENGED WORD GUIDE

Challenged Words and Phrases	Inferred Meaning	Context Clues

TYPES OF CONTEXT COMPLEX CLUES

Examples of context clues:

Definition: Defined when it appears

Compare/Synonym/Appositive: Paired with other words that have similar meaning

Inference: Not directly described; has to be implied from context

Classification: Defined by its relationship to known words

Word	Word in Context	Type of Clue

CLUE-GLUE WORD CARDS

Front of cards

means	is	describes	states
like	as if	and	differ
not	different	unlike	because
due to	if…then	consequently	whereas

Back of cards

definition	definition	definition	definition
compare	compare	compare	contrast
contrast	contrast	contrast	cause & effect
cause & effect	cause & effect	cause & effect	contrast

SEMANTIC GRADIENT

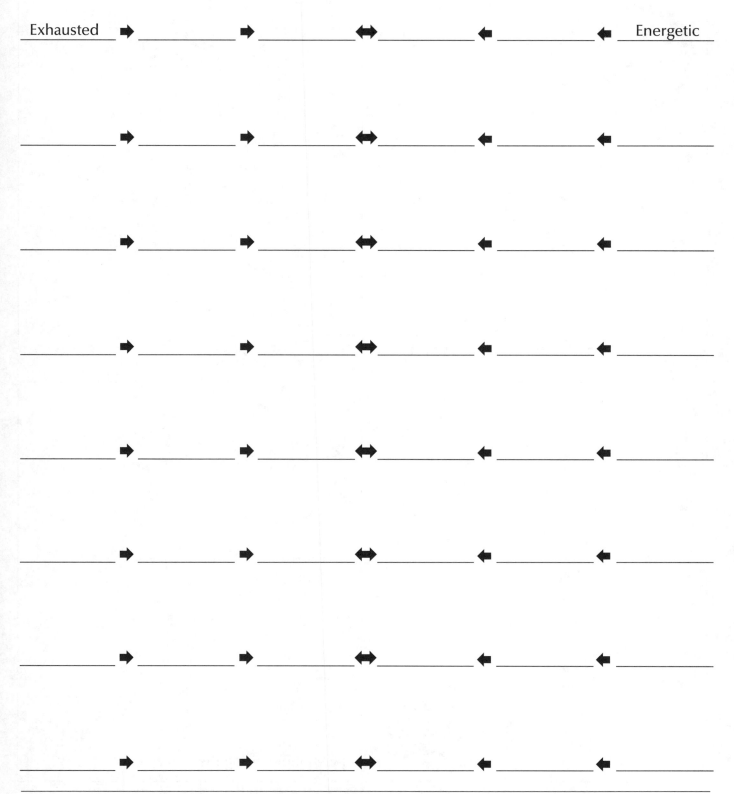

Exhausted ➡ _____ ➡ _____ ⬌ _____ ⬅ _____ ⬅ Energetic

FOUR CORNERS

What it is

NOT

Opposite

What it is...

Examples

Word

Connections

Illustrations using the letters

WORD SPLASH

Vocabulary Association

DEFINING MOMENT FEATURE CARDS

TEXT TRAITS

Examples of text features: Book layout

Terminology	Description
Title page	Gives the author's name, publisher, and places of publication
Copyright page	Tells when the book was printed
Table of contents	Lists page numbers for book contents and is found at the front of a text
Glossary	Lists definitions of terms and is found in the back of descriptive text
Bibliography	Gives appropriate credit for secondary sources of information from a given text
Index	Lists alphabetically words and terms from the book, sometimes with page numbers

Examples of text supports: Inside book

Terminology	Description
Bold words	Capture attention through use of darker font
Diagrams	Explain the text using simple pictures and sometimes words
Captions	Give descriptive information under an illustration or photograph
Graphs	Arrange information for comparison
Headings	Introduce new sections or chapters
Sidebars	Provide supplementary information on the side of the page

Examples of text structures: In the text

Terminology	Description	Signal Words/Phrases
Description	Provides information about a person, place, thing, idea, or concept	most important, to begin with, in fact, for example, to name a few
Sequential	Puts facts, events, or concepts in their order of occurrence (Time reference may be explicit or implicit.)	on (date), before, after, first, second, finally, subsequently, following, lastly
Compare and contrast	Identifies similarities and differences in facts, events, people, ideas, and concepts	similarly, like, in the same way, instead, on the contrary, as opposed to, conversely, unlike
Cause and effect	Describes facts, events, or concepts as the cause (Why did it happen?) that makes an effect (What happened?)	because, since, consequently, this led to, therefore, due to, then/so
Problem and solution	Illustrates development of a dilemma and provides one or more solutions to unravel the problem	this led to, as a result of, since the resolution is, nevertheless, so
Question and answer	Poses queries and leads the way to the answer through the facts, events, people, ideas, and concepts	how, when, what, why, who, it could be that, one may conclude, where, the best guess might be

Sustaining Strategic Readers: Techniques for Supporting Content Literacy in Grades 6–12 by Valerie Ellery and Jennifer L. Rosenboom.
© 2011 International Reading Association. May be copied for classroom use.

CONSTRUCTING STRUCTURE GUIDE

I think I will learn . . .

Title . . .

Headings / Subheadings . . .

What I know about the topic . . .

Questions I would like to have answered . . .

TEXT/CONCEPT CONNECTIONS PROMPTS

Text/Concept-to-Self
- That is interesting to me because....
- This relates to my experiences....
- This reminds me of....

Text/Concept-to-Text/Concept
- The (character[s], setting, events) are similar to another text....
- This is (similar to, different from) another text I have read....
- This reminds me of another text that I have read....

Text/Concept-to-World
- This was significant in the real world....
- The reading related to the world around me....
- This text (compares, contrasts) with current or historical world experiences....

PREDICTION BOXES GRID

Box 1: Convergent Thinking	Box 2: Making Connections	Box 3: Using Picture to Extend Prediction
Box 4: Revising Prediction	Box 5: Confirming Predictions	Box 6: Evaluating Performance

ANTICIPATION/REACTION GUIDE

Name:_____ Date:_____

Text: _____

Before Reading/Prediction	Statement	After Reading Reaction (Confirmed or Changed)
	1.	
	2.	
	3.	
	4.	
	5.	

MAIN IDEA WHEEL

Date:_____

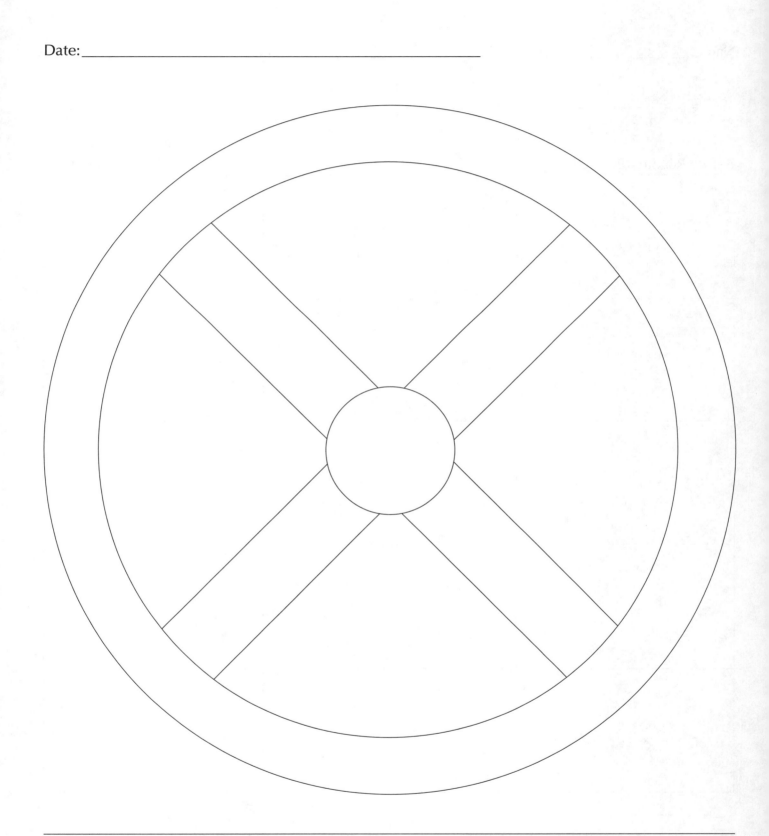

NARRATIVE PYRAMID

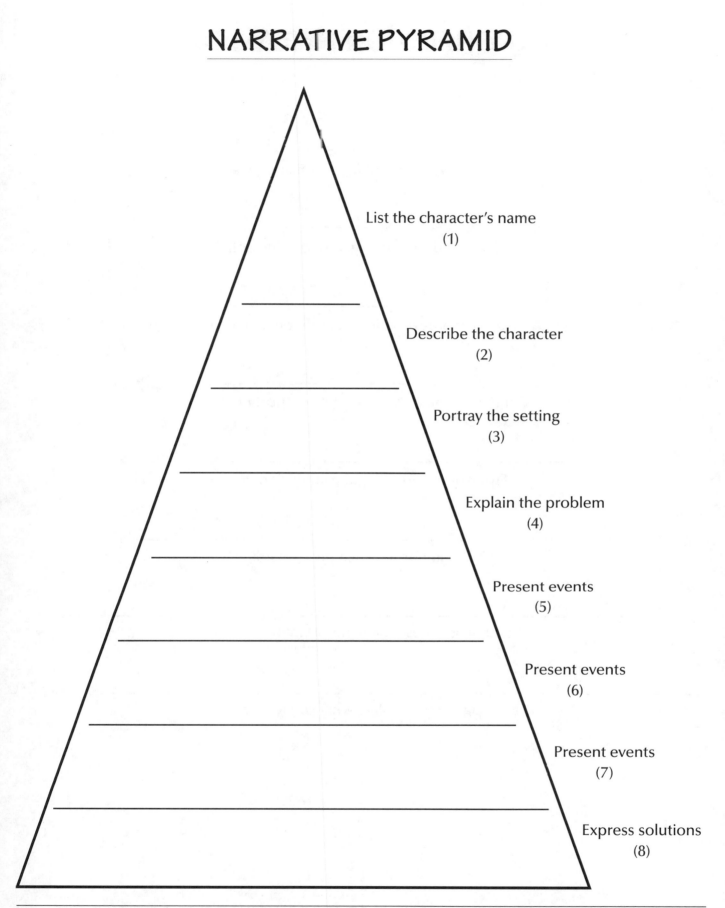

List the character's name
(1)

Describe the character
(2)

Portray the setting
(3)

Explain the problem
(4)

Present events
(5)

Present events
(6)

Present events
(7)

Express solutions
(8)

NONFICTION PYRAMID

_____
One word describing one major idea

_____ _____
Two words describing a supporting detail

_____ _____ _____
Three words describing another major idea

_____ _____ _____ _____
Four words describing another supporting detail

_____ _____ _____ _____ _____
Five words describing the author's purpose

_____ _____ _____ _____ _____ _____
Six important vocabulary words

_____ _____ _____ _____ _____ _____ _____
Seven words describing important reader's aids

_____ _____ _____ _____ _____ _____ _____ _____
Eight words telling what you learned

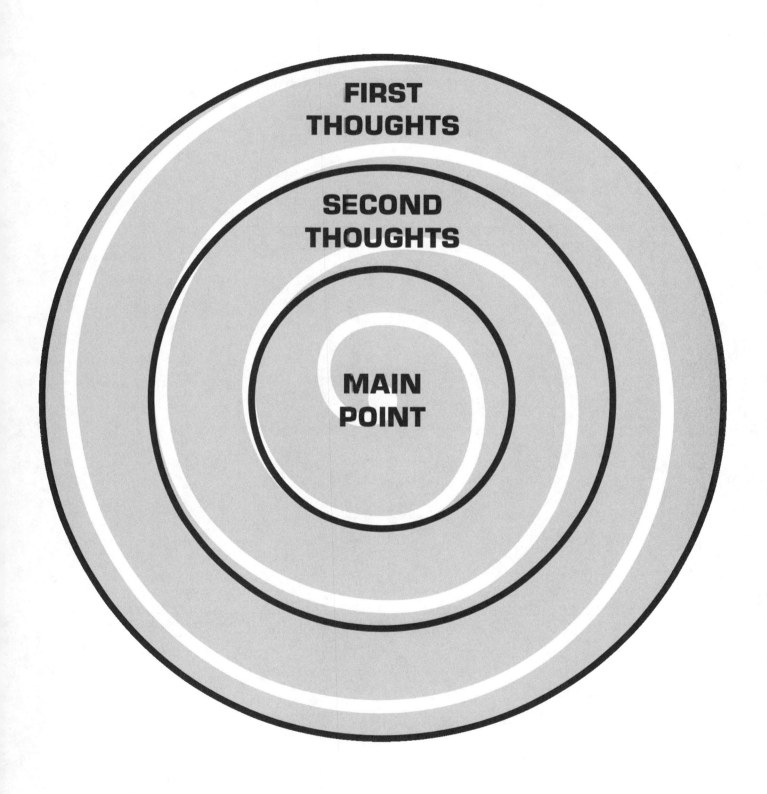

References

Afflerbach, P. (2007). *Understanding and using reading assessment, K–12*. Newark, DE: International Reading Association.

Allen, J. (2004). *Tools for teaching content literacy*. Portland, ME: Stenhouse.

Allen, J. (2007). *Inside words: Tools for teaching academic vocabulary, grades 4–12*. Portland, ME: Stenhouse.

Allington, R.L. (2001). *What really matters for struggling readers: Designing research-based programs*. New York: Longman.

Allington, R.L., & Walmsley, S.A. (Eds.). (2007). *No quick fix, the RTI edition: Rethinking literacy programs in America's elementary schools*. Newark, DE: International Reading Association; New York: Teachers College Press.

Amer, A. (2006). Reflections on Bloom's revised taxonomy. *Electronic Journal of Research in Educational Psychology, 4*(1), 213–230.

Amtmann, D., Abbott, R.D., & Berninger, V.W. (2008). Identifying and predicting classes of response to explicit phonological spelling instruction during independent composing. *Journal of Learning Disabilities, 41*(3), 218–234. doi:10.1177/0022219408315639

Anderson, L.W., & Krathwohl, D. (Eds.). (2001). *A taxonomy for learning, teaching, and assessing: A revision of Bloom's taxonomy of educational objectives*. New York: Longman.

Archer, A.L., Gleason, M.M., & Vachon, V. (2000). *REWARDS: Reading excellence word attack and rate development strategies*. Longmont, CO: Sopris West.

Athans, S.K., & Devine, D.A. (2010). *Fun-tastic activities for differentiating comprehension instruction, grades 2–6*. Newark, DE: International Reading Association.

Baldwin, R.S., Ford, J.C., & Readence, J.E. (1981). Teaching word connotations: An alternative strategy. *Reading World, 21*(2), 103–108.

Baumann, J.F., Font, G., Edwards, E.C., & Boland, E. (2005). Strategies for teaching middle-grade students to use word-part and context clues to expand reading vocabulary. In E.H. Hiebert & M.L. Kamil (Eds.), *Teaching and learning vocabulary: Bringing research to practice* (pp. 179–205). Mahwah, NJ: Erlbaum.

Bean, T.W., & Harper, H. (2009). The "adolescent" in adolescent literacy: A preliminary review. In K.D. Wood & W.E. Blanton (Eds.), *Literacy instruction for adolescents: Research-based practice* (pp. 37–53). New York: Guilford.

Bear, D.R., Invernizzi, M., Templeton, S., & Johnston, F. (2008). *Words their way: Word study for phonics, vocabulary, and spelling instruction* (4th ed.). Upper Saddle River, NJ: Prentice Hall.

Beaver, J., & Carter, M. (2003). *Developmental reading assessment, grades 4–8 (DRA2)* (2nd ed.). Parsippany, NJ: Celebration.

Beck, I.L., McKeown, M.G., & Kucan, L. (2008). *Creating robust vocabulary: Frequently asked questions and extended examples*. New York: Guilford.

Beers, K. (2003). *When kids can't read: What teachers can do*. Portsmouth, NH: Heinemann.

Berne, J.I., & Blachowicz, C.L.Z. (2008). What reading teachers say about vocabulary instruction: Voices from the classroom. *The Reading Teacher, 62*(4), 314–323. doi:10.1598/RT.62.4.4

Bhattacharya, A., & Ehri, L.C. (2004). Graphosyllabic analysis helps adolescent struggling readers read and spell words. *Journal of Learning Disabilities, 37*(4), 331–348. doi:10.1177/00222194040370040501

Biancarosa, C., & Snow, C.E. (2006). *Reading next—A vision for action and research in middle and high school literacy: A report to Carnegie Corporation of New York* (2nd ed.). Washington, DC: Alliance for Excellent Education.

Blachowicz, C.L.Z. (1986). Making connections: Alternatives to the vocabulary notebook. *Journal of Reading, 29*(7), 643–649.

Blachowicz, C.L.Z., & Fisher, P. (2006). *Teaching vocabulary in all classrooms* (3rd ed.). Upper Saddle River, NJ: Merrill/Prentice Hall.

Blevins, W. (2001). *Building fluency: Lessons and strategies for reading success.* New York: Scholastic.

Bloodgood, J.W., & Pacifici, L.C. (2004). Bringing word study to intermediate classrooms. *The Reading Teacher, 58*(3), 250–263.

Bloom B.S. (1956). *Taxonomy of educational objectives: The classification of educational goals.* New York: David McKay.

Brassell, D., & Rasinski, T.V. (2008). *Comprehension that works: Taking students beyond ordinary understanding to deep comprehension.* Huntington Beach, CA: Shell.

Bromley, K. (2007). Nine things every teacher should know about words and vocabulary instruction. *Journal of Adolescent & Adult Literacy, 50*(7), 528–537. doi:10.1598/JAAL.50.7.2

Brophy, J. (1983). Conceptualizing student motivation. *Educational Psychologist, 18*(3), 200–215.

Buehl, D. (2001). *Classroom strategies for interactive learning* (2nd ed.). Newark, DE: International Reading Association.

Buehl, D. (2009a). *Classroom strategies for interactive learning* (3rd ed.). Newark, DE: International Reading Association.

Buehl, D. (2009b). Mentoring literacy practices in academic classrooms. In S. Parris, D. Fisher, & K. Headley (Eds.), *Adolescent literacy, field tested: Effective solutions for every classroom* (pp. 228–238). Newark, DE: International Reading Association.

Caine, G., & Caine, R.N. (2007). *Natural learning: The basis for raising and sustaining high standards of real world performance.* Idyllwild, CA: The National Learning Research Institute. Retrieved August 1, 2010, from www.naturallearninginstitute.org/UPDATEDSITE/DOCUMENTS/POSITION_PAPER.pdf

Caldwell, J., & Ford, M.P. (2002). *Where have all the bluebirds gone? How to soar with flexible grouping.* Portsmouth, NH: Heinemann.

Cambourne, B. (1995). Toward an educationally relevant theory of literacy learning: Twenty years of inquiry. *The Reading Teacher, 49*(3), 182–190. doi:10.1598/RT.49.3.1

Campbell, K.U., & Mercer, C.D. (1998). *Great leaps reading program.* Gainesville, FL: Diarmuid.

Canter, A., Klotz, M.B., & Cowan, K. (2008). Response to intervention: The future for secondary schools. *Principal Leadership, 8*(6), 12–15. Retrieved June 29, 2010, from www.nasponline.org/resources/principals/RTI%20Part%201-NASSP%20February%202008.pdf

Caskey, M.M. (2008). Comprehension strategies that make a difference for struggling readers. In J. Lewis & S. Lenski (Eds.), *Reading success for struggling adolescent learners* (pp. 170–188). Newark, DE: International Reading Association.

Caskey, M.M., & Anfara, V.A., Jr. (2007). *Research summary: Young adolescents' developmental characteristics.* Westerville, OH: National Middle School Association. Retrieved July 1, 2010, from www.nmsa.org/Research/ResearchSummaries/DevelopmentalCharacteristics/tabid/1414/Default.aspx

Chen, H-C., & Graves, M.F. (1995). Effects of previewing and providing background knowledge on Taiwanese college students' comprehension of American short stories. *TESOL Quarterly, 29*(4), 663–686.

Coffield, F., Moseley, D., Hall, E., & Ecclestone, K. (2004). *Learning styles and pedagogy in post-16 learning: A systematic and critical review*. London: Learning and Skills Research Centre. Retrieved July 3, 2010, from www.hull.ac.uk/php/edskas/learning%20styles.pdf

Common Core State Standards Initiative. (2010). *The standards*. Retrieved June 20, 2010, from www.corestandards.org/the-standards

Crist, B.I. (1975). One capsule a week—a painless remedy for vocabulary ills. *Journal of Reading, 19*(2), 147–149.

Deshler, D.D., & Schumaker, J.B. (1988). An instructional model for teaching students how to learn. In J.L. Graden, J.E. Zins, & M.J. Curtis (Eds.), *Alternative educational delivery systems: Enhancing instructional options for all students* (pp. 391–411). Washington, DC: National Association of School Psychologists.

Dewey, J. (1913). *Interest and effort in education*. Boston: Riverside.

Drieghe, D., Pollatsek, A., Staub, A., & Rayner, K. (2008). The word grouping hypothesis and eye movements during reading. *Journal of Experimental Psychology, 34*(6), 1552–1560.

Duffy, G. (2009). *Explaining reading: A resource for teaching concepts, skills, and strategies* (2nd ed.). New York: Guilford.

Duffy, H. (2007). *Meeting the needs of significantly struggling learners in high school: A look at approaches to tiered intervention*. Washington, DC: National High School Center. Retrieved May 10, 2010, from www.betterhighschools.org/docs/NHSC_RTIBrief_08-02-07.pdf

Duke, N.K., & Pearson, P.D. (2002). Effective practices for developing reading comprehension. In A.E. Farstrup & S.J. Samuels (Eds.), *What research has to say about reading instruction* (3rd ed., pp. 205–242). Newark, DE: International Reading Association.

Ebbers, S.M., & Denton, C.A. (2008). A root awakening: Vocabulary instruction for older students with reading difficulties. *Learning Disabilities Research & Practice, 23*(2), 90–102. doi:10.1111/j.1540-5826.2008.00267.x

Eber, P. (2007). Assessing student learning: Applying Bloom's taxonomy. *Human Service Education, 27*(1), 45–53.

Edwards, P.A., Turner, J.D., & Mokhtari, K. (2008). Balancing the assessment *of* learning and *for* learning in support of student literacy achievement. *The Reading Teacher, 61*(8), 682–684. doi:10.1598/RT.61.8.12

Ehren, B.J., & Laster, B.P. (2010). *RTI Webinar: RTI at the secondary level, Looking on the bright side*. Retrieved July 15, 2010, from www.reading.org/Libraries/Resources/RTI_at_the_secondary_level.sflb.ashx

Ellery, V. (2005). *Creating strategic readers: Techniques for developing competency in phonemic awareness, phonics, fluency, vocabulary, and comprehension*. Newark, DE: International Reading Association.

Ellery, V. (2009). *Creating strategic readers: Techniques for developing competency in phonemic awareness, phonics, fluency, vocabulary, and comprehension* (2nd ed.). Newark, DE: International Reading Association.

Farstrup, A.E., & Samuels, S.J. (2002). *What research has to say about reading instruction* (3rd ed.). Newark, DE: International Reading Association.

Fawcett, G., & Rasinski, T.V. (2008). Fluency strategies for struggling adolescent readers. In J. Lewis & S. Lenski (Eds.), *Reading success for struggling adolescent learners* (pp. 155–168). New York: Guilford.

Fink, R., & Samuels, J. (Eds.). (2008). *Inspiring reading success: Interest and motivation in an age of high-stakes testing*. Newark, DE: International Reading Association.

Fisher, D., Frey, N., & Lapp, D. (2009). *In a reading state of mind: Brain research, teacher modeling, and comprehension instruction*. Newark, DE: International Reading Association.

Fountas, I., & Pinnell, G. (2001). *Guiding readers and writers, grades 3–6: Teaching comprehension, genre, and content literacy*. Portsmouth, NH: Heinemann.

Frayer, D., Frederick, W.C., & Klausmeier, H.J. (1969). *A schema for testing the level of cognitive mastery*. Madison, WI: Wisconsin Center for Education Research.

Frey, N., & Fisher, D. (2004). Using graphic novels, anime, and the Internet in an urban high school. *English Journal, 93*(3), 19–25.

Fuchs, L.S., & Fuchs, D. (2008). Progress monitoring within a multi-tiered prevention system: Best practices. In J. Grimes & A. Thomas (Eds.), *Best practices in school psychology* (Vol. 5, pp. 2147–2164). Bethesda, MD: National Association of School Psychologists.

Fuchs, L.S., Fuchs, D., Hosp, M.K., & Jenkins, J.R. (2001). Oral reading fluency as an indicator of reading competence: A theoretical, empirical, and historical analysis. *Scientific Studies of Reading, 5*(3), 239–256. doi:10.1207/S1532799XSSR0503_3

Gardner, H. (1993). *Frames of mind: The theory of multiple intelligences* (10th anniv. ed.). New York: Basic.

Gardner, H. (1999). *Intelligence reframed: Multiple intelligences for the 21st century*. New York: Basic.

Gaskins, I., Ehri, L.C., Cress, C., O'Hara, C., & Donnelly, K. (1996). Procedures for word learning: Making discoveries about words. *The Reading Teacher, 50*(4), 312–327.

Gill, S. (2008). The comprehension matrix: A tool for designing comprehension instruction. *The Reading Teacher, 62*(2), 106–113.

Goatley, V.J., & Raphael, T.E. (1992). Non-traditional learners' written and dialogic response to literature. In J. Zutell & S. McCormick (Eds.), *Fortieth yearbook of the national reading conference* (pp. 313–322). Chicago: National Reading Conference.

Godbey, G. (2008). *Leisure in your life: New perspectives*. State College, PA: Venture.

Graves, M.F. (2006). *The vocabulary book: Learning and instruction*. New York: Teachers College Press; Newark, DE: International Reading Association; Urbana, IL: National Council of Teachers of English.

Graves, M.F. (2007). Vocabulary instruction in the middle grades. *Voices from the Middle, 15*(1), 13–19.

Graves, M.F. (2009). *Teaching individual words: One size does not fit all*. New York: Teachers College Press; Newark, DE: International Reading Association.

Graves, M.F., & Cooke, C.L. (1980). Effects of previewing difficult short stories for high school students. *Research on Reading in Secondary Schools, 6*, 38–54.

Graves, M.F., Cooke, C.L., & Laberge, M.J. (1983). Effects of previewing difficult short stories on low ability junior high school students' comprehension recall, and attitudes. *Reading Research Quarterly, 18*(3), 262–276. doi:10.2307/747388

Graves, M.F., Juel, C., & Graves, B.B. (1998). *Teaching reading in the 21st century*. Boston: Allyn & Bacon.

Graves, M.F., & Watts-Taffe, S. (2008). For the love of words: Fostering word consciousness in young readers. *The Reading Teacher, 62*(3), 185–193. doi:10.1598/RT.62.3.1

Greene, F. (1979). Radio reading. In C. Pennock (Ed.), *Reading comprehension at four linguistic levels* (pp. 104–107). Newark, DE: International Reading Association.

Greenwood, S.C., & Flanigan, K. (2007). Overlapping vocabulary and comprehension: Context clues complement semantic gradients. *The Reading Teacher, 61*(3), 249–254. doi:10.1598/RT.61.3.5

Harackiewicz, J.M., Durik, A.M., Barron, K.E., Linnenbrink-Garcia, L., & Tauer, J.M. (2008). The role of achievement goals in the development of interest: Reciprocal relations between achievement goals, interest, and performance. *Journal of Educational Psychology, 100*(1), 105–122. doi:10.1037/0022-0663.100.1.105

Harmon, J.M., Hedrick, W.B., & Wood, K.D. (2005). Research on vocabulary instruction in the content areas: Implications for struggling readers. *Reading & Writing Quarterly, 21(3)*, 261–280.

Harmon, J.M., Wood, K.D., & Hedrick, W.B. (2006). *Instructional strategies for teaching content vocabulary, grades 4–12*. Westerville, OH: National Middle School Association; Newark, DE: International Reading Association.

Harris, L.A. (2007). Adolescent literacy: Wordy study with middle and high school students. *TEACHING Exceptional Children Plus, 3*(4). Retrieved January 11, 2011, from escholarship.bc.edu/education/tecplus/vol3/iss4/art4

Harste, J.C., Short, K.C., & Burke, C.L. (1988). *Creating classrooms for authors: The reading-writing connection.* Portsmouth, NH: Heinemann.

Harvey, S., & Goudvis, A. (2000). *Strategies that work: Teaching comprehension to enhance understanding.* Portland, ME: Stenhouse.

Harvey, S., & Goudvis, A. (2007). *Strategies that work: Teaching comprehension for understanding and engagement* (2nd ed.). Portland, ME: Stenhouse.

Hasbrouck, J., & Tindal, G. (2006). Oral reading fluency norms: A valuable assessment tool for reading teachers. *The Reading Teacher, 59*(7), 636–644.

Hedrick, W.B., Harmon, J.M., & Wood, K. (2008). Prominent content vocabulary strategies and what secondary preservice teachers think about them. *Reading Psychology, 29*(5), 443–470. doi:10.1080/02702710802275330

Heimlich, J.E., & Pittelman, S.D. (1986). *Semantic mapping: Classroom applications.* Newark, DE: International Reading Association.

Hennings, D.G. (2000). Contextually relevant word study: Adolescent vocabulary development across the curriculum. *Journal of Adolescent & Adult Literacy, 44*(3), 268–279.

Herber, H. (1978). *Teaching reading in content areas* (2nd ed.). Englewood Cliffs, NJ: Prentice Hall.

Herber, H., & Nelson-Herber, J. (1987). Developing independent learners. *Journal of Reading, 30*(7), 584–588.

Herron, J. (2008). Why phonics teaching must change. *Educational Leadership, 66*(1), 77–81.

Hibbing, A.N., & Rankin-Erickson, J.L. (2003). A picture is worth a thousand words: Using visual images to improve comprehension for middle school struggling readers. *The Reading Teacher, 56*(8), 758–770.

Hiebert, E.H. (2005). *QuickReads.* Upper Saddle River, NJ: Pearson.

Hilden, K.R., & Pressley, M. (2007). Self-regulation through transactional strategies instruction. *Reading & Writing Quarterly, 23*(1), 51–75. doi:10.1080/10573560600837651

Hodgkinson, H. (2006). *The whole child in a fractured world.* For the Commission on the Whole Child convened by Association for Supervision and Curriculum Development. Alexandria, VA: Association for Supervision and Curriculum Development. Retrieved March, 15, 2009, from www.ascd.org/ASCD/pdf/fracturedworld.pdf

Hoyt, L. (1992). Many ways of knowing: Using drama, oral interactions, and visual arts to enhance reading comprehension. *The Reading Teacher, 45*(8), 580–584.

Hyerle, D.N. (2004). *Student successes with thinking maps: School-based research, results, and models for achievement using visual tools.* Thousand Oaks, CA: Corwin.

International Reading Association. (2008, December/January). IRA offers policy recommendations to U.S. President-elect Barack Obama. *Reading Today, 26*(3), 1, 4, 5.

International Reading Association Response to Intervention Commission. (2010). *Response to intervention: Guiding principles for educators from the International Reading Association.* Newark, DE: Authors. Retrieved June 30, 2010, from www.reading.org/Libraries/Resources/RTI_brochure_web.sflb.ashx

Irvin, J., Meltzer, J., Dean, N., & Mickler, M.J. (2010). *Taking the lead on adolescent literacy: Action steps for schoolwide success.* Thousand Oaks, CA: Corwin; Newark, DE: International Reading Association.

Irvin, J.L., Meltzer, J., Mickler, M.J., Phillips, M., & Dean, N. (2009). *Meeting the challenge of adolescent literacy: Practical ideas for literacy leaders.* Newark, DE: International Reading Association.

Irwin, J.W. (1991). *Teaching reading comprehension processes* (2nd ed.). Englewood Cliffs, NJ: Prentice Hall.

Istifci, I. (2010). Playing with words: A study on word association responses. *Journal of International Social Research, 3*(10), 360–368.

Jang, H. (2008). Supporting students' motivation, engagement, and learning during an uninteresting activity. *Journal of Educational Psychology, 100*(4), 798–811. doi:10.1037/a0012841

Jensen, E. (2005). *Teaching with the brain in mind* (2nd ed.). Alexandria, VA: Association for Supervision and Curriculum Development.

Jensen, E., & Nickelsen, L. (2008). *Deeper learning: 7 powerful strategies for in-depth and longer-lasting learning.* Thousand Oaks, CA: Corwin.

Jewitt, C., & Kress, G. (Eds.). (2003). *Multimodal literacy.* London: Peter Lang.

Johns, J.L., & Berglund, R.L. (2006). *Fluency strategies and assessments.* Dubuque, IA: Kendall/Hunt.

Johns, J.L., & Berglund, R.L. (2010). *Fluency: Differentiated interventions and progress-monitoring assessments* (4th ed.). Dubuque, IA: Kendall/Hunt.

Johnson, E., Mellard, D.F., Fuchs, D., & McKnight, M.A. (2006). *Responsiveness to intervention (RTI): How to do it.* Lawrence, KS: National Research Center on Learning Disabilities.

Johnston, A.M., Barnes, M.A., & Desrochers, A. (2008). Reading comprehension: Developmental processes, individual differences, and interventions. *Canadian Psychology, 49*(2), 125–132.

Johnston, F., Invernizzi, M., Bear, D.R., & Templeton, S. (2009). *Words their way: Word sorts for syllables and affixes spellers* (2nd ed.). Boston: Pearson.

Johnston, P.H. (2010). A framework for response to intervention in literacy. In P.H. Johnston (Ed.), *RTI in Literacy—Responsive and Comprehensive* (pp. 1–9). Newark, DE: International Reading Association.

Kamil, M.L. (2003). *Adolescents and literacy: Reading for the 21st century.* Washington, DC: Alliance for Excellent Education.

Kane, S. (2007). *Literacy & learning in the content areas* (2nd ed.). Scottsdale, AZ: Holcomb Hathaway.

Keene, E.O., & Zimmermann, S. (2007). *Mosaic of thought: The power of comprehension strategy instruction.* (2nd ed.). Portsmouth, NH: Heinemann.

Kelly, M.J., & Clausen-Grace, N. (2007). *Comprehension shouldn't be silent: From strategy instruction to student independence.* Newark, DE: International Reading Association.

Kieffer, M.J., & Lesaux, N.K. (2007). Breaking down words to build meaning: Morphology, vocabulary, and reading comprehension in the urban classroom. *The Reading Teacher, 61*(2), 134–144. doi:10.1598/RT.61.2.3

Kinniburgh, L., & Shaw, E., Jr. (2007). Building reading fluency in elementary science through readers' theatre. *Science Activities, 44*(1), 16–22. doi:10.3200/SATS.44.1.16-22

Klauda, S.L., & Guthrie, J.T. (2008). Relationships of three components of reading fluency to reading comprehension. *Journal of Educational Psychology, 100*(2), 310–321. doi:10.1037/0022-0663.100.2.310

Kohn, A. (1993). *Punished by rewards: The trouble with gold stars, incentive plans, A's, praise, and other bribes.* Boston: Houghton Mifflin.

Kohn, A. (2005). Unconditional teaching. *Educational Leadership, 63*(1), 20–24.

Kossack, S. (2007). Comparing the effects of high and low learning pathway instructional approaches on vocabulary mastery of middle school at-risk learners. *The International Journal of Learning, 14*(6), 199–206.

Kunen, S., Cohen, R., & Solman, R. (1981). A levels-of-processing analysis of Bloom's taxonomy. *Journal of Educational Psychology, 73*(2), 202–211. doi:10.1037/0022-0663.73.2.202

Lapp, D., & Fisher, D. (2009). *Essential readings on comprehension.* Newark, DE: International Reading Association.

Lavoie, R. (2007). *The motivation breakthrough: 6 secrets to turning on the tuned-out child*. New York: Touchstone.

Lee, C.D., & Spratley, A. (2010). *Reading in the disciplines: The challenges of adolescent literacy*. New York: Carnegie Corporation of New York.

Lenski, S.D., & Lewis, J. (2008). *Reading success for struggling adolescent learners*. New York: Guilford.

Lenz, B.K., & Hughes, C.A. (1990). A word identification strategy for adolescents with learning disabilities. *Journal of Learning Disabilities, 23*(3), 149–158. doi:10.1177/002221949002300304

Lesaux, N., & Kieffer, M. (2010). Exploring sources of reading comprehension difficulties among language minority learners and their classmates in early adolescence. *American Educational Research Journal, 47*(3), 596–632. doi:10.3102/0002831209355469

Leslie, M., & Caldwell, J. (2005). *Qualitative reading inventory-4* (4th ed.). Boston: Allyn & Bacon.

Levine, M. (2002). *A mind at a time*. New York: Simon & Schuster.

Manzo, A.V. (1969). The ReQuest procedure. *Journal of Reading, 13*(2), 123–126.

Manzo, U.C., & Manzo, A.V. (2008). Teaching vocabulary-learning strategies: Word consciousness, word connection, and word prediction. In A. Farstrup & S. Samuel (Eds.), *What research has to say about vocabulary instruction* (pp. 80–105). Newark, DE: International Reading Association.

Marcell, B.T. (2010). Put the brakes on NASCAR reading. *Educational Leadership, 67*(6). Retrieved June 3, 2010, from www.ascd.org/publications/educational-leadership/mar10/vol67/num06/Put-the-Brakes-on-NASCAR-Reading.aspx

Martin, G.L. (2004). Encoder: A connectionist model of how learning to visually encode fixated text images improves reading fluency. *Psychological Review, 112*(4), 814–840.

Marzano, R.J. (2004). *Building background knowledge for academic achievement: Research on what works in schools*. Alexandria, VA: Association for Supervision and Curriculum Development.

Marzano, R.J. (2010). *Formative assessment & standards-based grading*. Bloomington, IN: Solution Tree.

Marzano, R.J., & Pickering, D. (2005). *Building academic vocabulary: Teacher's manual*. Alexandria, VA: Association for Supervision and Curriculum Development.

Marzano, R.J., Pickering, D., & Pollock, J.E. (2001). *Classroom instruction that works: Research-based strategies for increasing student achievement*. Alexandria, VA: Association for Supervision and Curriculum Development.

Maslow, A.H. (1943). A theory of human motivation. *Psychological Review, 50*(4), 370–396. doi:10.1037/h0054346

McGinley, W.J, & Denner, P.R. (1987). Story impressions: A prereading/writing activity. *Journal of Reading, 31*(3), 248–253.

McKeown, M.G., Beck, I.L., & Blake, R.G.K. (2009). Rethinking reading comprehension instruction: A comparison of instruction for strategies and content approaches. *Reading Research Quarterly, 44*(3), 218–253.

McKeown, M.G., Beck, I.L., Sinatra, G.M., & Loxterman, J.A. (1992). The contribution of prior knowledge and coherent text to comprehension. *Reading Research Quarterly, 27*(1), 78–93.

McNamara, D.S., Ozuru, Y., Best, R., & O'Reilly, T. (2007). The 4-pronged comprehension strategy framework. In D.S. McNamara (Ed.), *Reading comprehension strategies: Theories, interventions, and technologies* (pp. 465–496). Mahwah, NJ: Erlbaum.

McNaught, C., & Lam, P. (2010). Using Wordle as a supplementary research tool. *The Qualitative Report, 15*(3), 630–643. Retrieved July 10, 2010, from www.nova.edu/ssss/QR/QR15-3/mcnaught.pdf

Merton, R.K. (1968). The Matthew effect in science: The reward and communication systems of science are considered. *Science, 159*(3810), 56–63.

Miller, P., & Eilam, B. (2008). Development in the thematic and containment-relation-oriented organization of word concepts. *The Journal of Educational Research, 101*(6), 350–361. doi:10.3200/JOER.101.6.350-362

Montelongo, J.A. (2008). Text guides: Scaffolding summarization and fortifying reading skills. *International Journal of Learning, 15*(7), 289–296.

Moore, D.W. (2009). Advocating reading instruction in middle and high school classrooms. In K.D. Wood & W.E. Blanton (Eds.), *Literacy instruction for adolescents: Research-based practice* (pp. 13–36). New York: Guilford.

Mraz, M., Rickelman, R.J., & Vacca, R.T. (2009). Content-area reading: Past, present, and future. In K.D. Wood & W.E. Blanton (Eds.), *Literacy instruction for adolescents: Research-based practice* (pp. 77–91). New York: Guilford.

Nagy, W.E. (1988). *Teaching vocabulary to improve reading comprehension*. Newark, DE: International Reading Association; Urbana, IL: National Council of Teachers of English.

Nagy, W.E., Diakidoy, I.N., & Anderson, R.C. (1991). *The development of knowledge of derivational suffixes* (Tech. Rep. No. 536). Champaign, IL: Center for the Study of Reading.

Nagy, W.E., & Scott, J.A. (2000). Vocabulary processes. In M.L. Kamil, P. Mosenthal, P.D. Pearson, & R. Barr (Eds.), *Handbook of reading research* (Vol. 3, pp. 269–284). Mahwah, NJ: Erlbaum.

Nathan, R.G., & Stanovich, K.E. (1991). The causes and consequences of differences in reading fluency. *Theory into Practice, 30*(3), 176–184. doi:10.1080/00405849109543498

National Assessment of Educational Progress. (2009). *The nation's report card*. Retrieved August 10, 2010, from nationsreportcard.gov/reading_2009/summary_g12.asp

National Association of State Boards of Education. (2006). *Reading at risk: The state response to the crisis in adolescent literacy* (Rev. ed.). Alexandria, VA: Author.

National Center on Response to Intervention. (2010). *Essential components of RTI: A closer look at Response to Intervention*. Retrieved August 10, 2010, from www.rti4success.org/images/stories/pdfs/rtiessential components_051310.pdf

National Council of Teachers of English. (2004). *Framing statements on assessment*. Retrieved June 3, 2010, from www.ncte.org/positions/statements/assessmentframingst

National Council of Teachers of English. (2006). *NCTE principles of adolescent literacy reform: A policy research brief*. Retrieved March 1, 2011, from www.ncte.org/library/NCTEFiles/Resources/Positions/ Adol-Lit-Brief.pdf

National Geographic School Publishing. (2008). *Inside: Language, literacy, and content*. Carmel, CA: Hampton-Brown.

National Governors Association Center for Best Practices and Council of Chief State School Officers. (2010). National Governors Association and state education chiefs launch common state academic standards. Retrieved May 29, 2010, from www.nga.org/portal/site/nga/menuitem.6c9a8a9ebc6ae07eee28aca9501 010a0/?vgnextoid=99e3370b240e8210VgnVCM1000005e00100aRCRD&vgnextchannel=759b8f20053 61010VgnVCM1000001a01010aRCRD

National High School Center, National Center on Response to Intervention, and Center on Instruction. (2010). *Tiered interventions in high schools: Using preliminary "lessons learned" to guide ongoing discussion*. Washington, DC: American Institutes for Research.

National Institute of Child Health and Human Development. (2000). *Report of the National Reading Panel. Teaching children to read: An evidence-based assessment of the scientific research literature on reading and its implications for reading instruction* (NIH Publication No. 00–4769). Washington, DC: U.S. Government Printing Office.

National Institute for Literacy. (2007). *What content-area teachers should know about adolescent literacy.* Retrieved June 30, 2010, from www.cdl.org/resource-library/pdf/what_contentarea_teachers_should_know_about_al.pdf

Nelson, D.L. (2008). A context-based strategy for teaching vocabulary. *English Journal, 97*(4), 33–37.

Newkirk, T. (2010). The case for slow reading. *Educational Leadership, 67*(6), 6–11.

Nokes, J.D. (2008). The observation/inference chart: Improving students' abilities to make inferences while reading nontraditional texts. *Journal of Adolescent & Adult Literacy, 51*(7), 538–546. doi:10.1598/JAAL.51.7.2

Nye, B., Konstantopoulos, S., & Hedges, L.V. (2004). How large are teacher effects? *Educational Evaluation and Policy Analysis, 26*(3), 237–257. doi:10.3102/01623737026003237

O'Connor, P.J., & Jackson, C.J. (2008). The factor structure and validity of the learning styles profiler. *European Journal of Psychological Assessment, 24*(2), 117–123. doi:10.1027/1015-5759.24.2.117

O'Connor, R.E., White, A., & Swanson, H.L. (2007). Repeated reading versus continuous reading: Influences on reading fluency and comprehension. *Council for Exceptional Children, 74*(1), 31–46.

Ogle, D.M. (2000). Make it visual: A picture is worth a thousand words. In M. McLaughlin & M. Vogt (Eds.), *Creativity and innovation in content area teaching* (pp. 55–71). Norwood, MA: Christopher-Gordon.

Onofrey, K.A, & Theurer, J.L. (2007). What's a teacher to do: Suggestions for comprehension strategy instruction. *The Reading Teacher, 60*(7), 681–684.

Opitz, M., & Rasinski, T.V. (2008). *Good-bye round robin: 25 effective oral reading strategies* (Updated ed.). Portsmouth, NH: Heinemann.

Padak, N., Newton, E., Rasinski, T.V., & Newton, R.M. (2008). Getting to the root of word study: Teaching Latin and Greek word roots in elementary and middle grades. In A.E. Farstrup & S.J. Samuels (Eds.), *What research has to say about vocabulary instruction* (pp. 6–31). Newark, DE: International Reading Association.

Paris, S.G., Wasik, B.A., & Turner, J.C. (1991). The development of strategic readers. In R. Barr, M.L. Kamil, P. Mosenthal, & P.D. Pearson (Eds.), *Handbook of reading research* (Vol. 2, pp. 609–640). White Plains, NY: Longman.

Parris, S.R., Fisher, D., & Headley K. (Eds.). (2009). *Adolescent literacy, field tested: Effective solutions for every classroom.* Newark, DE: International Reading Association.

Parsons, S.A. (2008). Providing all students ACCESS to self-regulated literacy learning. *The Reading Teacher, 61*(8), 628–635. doi:10.1598/RT.61.8.4

Pearson, P.D., & Gallagher, M.C. (1983). The instruction of reading comprehension. *Contemporary Educational Psychology, 8*(3), 317–344.

Pearson, P.D., Hiebert, E.H., & Kamil, M.L. (2007). Vocabulary assessment: What we know and what we need to learn. *Reading Research Quarterly, 42*(2), 282–296.

Petit, M. (2003, January). *Bridging the gap between large-scale and classroom assessment.* Presentation at the meeting of the National Research Council, Washington, DC.

Pinnell, G.S., Pikulski, J.J., Wixson, K.K., Campbell, J.R., Gough, P.B., & Beatty, A.S. (1995). *Listening to children read aloud data from NAEP's integral reading performance record CIRPR at grade 4* (Report No. 23-FR-04 prepared by the Educational Testing Service). Washington, DC: Office of Educational Research and Improvement, U.S. Department of Education.

Pittelman, S.D., Heimlich, J.E., Berglund, R.L., & French, M.P. (1991). *Semantic feature analysis: Classroom applications.* Newark, DE: International Reading Association.

Raphael, T.E. (1986). Teaching question answer relationships, revisited. *The Reading Teacher, 39*(6), 516–522.

Raphael, T.E., Highfield, K., & Au, K.H. (2006). *QAR now: A powerful and practical framework that develops comprehension and higher-level thinking in all students.* New York: Scholastic.

Rasinski, T.V. (2000). Speed does matter in reading. *The Reading Teacher, 54*(2), 146–150.

Rasinski, T.V. (2006). Reading fluency instruction: Moving beyond accuracy, automaticity, and prosody. *The Reading Teacher, 59*(7), 704–706.

Rasinski, T.V., & Fawcett, G. (2008). Fluency for adolescent readers: The research we have, the research we need. In M.W. Conley, J.R. Freidhoff, M.B. Sherry, & S.F. Tuckey (Eds.), *Meeting the challenge of adolescent literacy: Research we have, research we need* (pp. 1–10). New York: Guilford.

Rasinski, T.V., Homan, S., & Biggs, M. (2009). Teaching reading fluency to struggling reading: Method, materials, and evidence. *Reading & Writing Quarterly, 25*(2–3), 192–204. doi:10.1080/10573560802683622

Rasinski, T.V., & Padak, N. (2005). *3-minute reading assessments: Word recognition, fluency, and comprehension, grades 5–8.* New York: Scholastic.

Readence, J.E., Bean, T., & Baldwin, R.S. (1981). *Content area reading: An integrated approach.* Dubuque, IA: Kendall/Hunt.

Readence, J.E., Bean, T.W., & Baldwin, R.S. (2008). *Content area reading: An integrated approach* (9th ed.). Dubuque, IA: Kendall/Hunt.

Rebora, A. (2010, April 9). Responding to RTI [Interview]. *Teacher Magazine, 3,* 12. Retrieved July 2, 2010, from www.edweek.org/tsb/articles/2010/04/12/02allington.h03.html?cmp=clpedweek&print=1

Redfield, D.L., & Rousseau, E.W. (1981). A meta-analysis of experimental research on teacher questioning behavior. *Review of Educational Research, 51*(2), 237–245.

Rozalski, M.E. (2010). *Response to Intervention: A rural high school's attempt to improve reading achievement.* Council for Exceptional Children. Retrieved June 28, 2010, from www.cec.sped.org/AM/Template.cfm?Section=CEC_Today1&TEMPLATE=/CM/ContentDisplay.cfm&CONTENTID=11753

Samuels, S.J., & Farstrup, A.E. (Eds.). (2006). *What research has to say about reading instruction* (3rd ed.). Newark, DE: International Reading Association.

Santa, C.M. (2006). A vision for adolescent literacy: Ours or theirs? *Journal of Adolescent & Adult Literacy, 49*(6), 466–476.

Santa, C.M., Havens, L.T, & Valdes, B.J. (2004). *Project CRISS: Creating independence through student-owned strategies* (3rd ed.). Dubuque, IA: Kendall/Hunt.

Scammacca, N., & Roberts, G., Vaughn. S., Edmonds, M., Wexler, J., Reutebuch, C.K., et al. (2007). *Interventions for adolescent struggling readers: A meta-analysis with implications for practice.* Portsmouth, NH: RMC Research Corporation, Center on Instruction. Retrieved July 30, 2010, from www.centeroninstruction.org/files/COI%20Struggling%20Readers.pdf

Schallert, D.L. (1982). The significance of knowledge: A synthesis of research related to schema theory. In W. Otto & S. White (Eds.), *Reading expository prose* (pp. 13–48). New York: Academic.

Schmidt, B., & Buckley, M. (1990). Plot relationships chart. In J.M. Bacon, D. Bewell, & M. Vogt (Eds.), *Responses to literature: Grades K–8* (pp. 7–8). Newark, DE: International Reading Association.

Schmidt, H.G., & Patel, V.L. (1987, April). *Effects of prior knowledge activation through small-group discussion on the processing of science text.* Paper presented at the annual meeting of the American Educational Research Association, Washington, DC.

Schwartz, S., & Bone, M. (1995). *Retelling, relating, reflecting: Beyond the 3 R's.* Toronto, ON, Canada: Nelson Thompson Learning.

Searfoss, L. (1975). Radio reading. *The Reading Teacher, 29*(3), 295–296.

Shanahan, T., & Shanahan, C. (2008). Teaching disciplinary literacy to adolescents: Rethinking content-area literacy. *Harvard Educational Review, 78*(1), 40–59.

Sharp, A.C., Sinatra, G.M., & Reynolds, R.E. 2008). The development of children's orthographic knowledge: A microgenetic perspective. *Reading Research Quarterly, 43*(3), 206–226. doi:10.1598/RRQ.43.3.1

Shepard, A. (1994). From script to stage: Tips for Readers Theatre. *The Reading Teacher, 48*(2), 184–185.

Silver, H.F., Strong, R.W., & Perini, M.J. (2001). *Tools for promoting active, in-depth learning* (2nd ed.). Woodbridge, NJ: Thoughtful Education.

Skinner, E.A., & Belmont, M.J. (1993). Motivation in the classroom: Reciprocal effects of teacher behavior and student engagement across the school year. *Journal of Educational Psychology, 85*(4), 571–581. doi:10.1037/0022-0663.85.4.571

Sloyer, S. (1982). *Readers Theatre: Story dramatization in the classroom.* Urbana, IL: National Council of Teachers of English.

Small, M. (2010). Beyond one right answer. *Educational Leadership, 68*(1), 28–32.

Smith, M., & Wilhelm, J. (2002). *Reading don't fix no Chevy's: Literacy in the lives of young men.* Portsmouth, NH: Heinemann.

Spires, H.A., & Donley, J. (1998). Prior knowledge activation: Inducing engagement with informational texts. *Journal of Educational Psychology, 90*(2), 249–260. doi:10.1037/0022-0663.90.2.249

Sprenger, M. (2005). *How to teach so students remember.* Alexandria, VA: Association for Supervision and Curriculum Development.

Stahl, S.A., & Nagy, W.E. (2006). *Teaching word meanings.* Mahwah, NJ: Erlbaum.

Stanovich, K.E. (1986). Matthew effects in reading: Some consequences of individual differences in the acquisition of literacy. *Reading Research Quarterly, 21*(4), 360–407. doi:10.1598/RRQ.21.4.1

Stiggins, R., & Chappuis, J. (2008). Enhancing student learning. *District Administrator, 44*(1), 42–44.

Strickland, D.S., Ganske, K., & Monroe, J.K. (2002). *Supporting struggling readers and writers: Strategies for classroom intervention, 3–6.* Portland, ME: Stenhouse; Newark, DE: International Reading Association.

Stull, A.T., & Mayer, R.E. (2007). Learning by doing versus learning by viewing: Three experimental comparisons of learner-generated versus author-provided graphic organizers. *Journal of Educational Psychology, 99*(4), 808–820. doi:10.1037/0022-0663.99.4.808

Tatum, A.W. (2008). *Best practices in secondary education: Reading fluency.* Des Moines, IA: National Geographic School Publishing/Hampton-Brown.

Taylor, B.M. (2008). Tier I: Effective classroom reading instruction in the elementary grades. In D. Fuchs, L. Fuchs, & S. Vaughn (Eds.), *Response to intervention: A framework for reading educators* (pp. 5–26). Newark, DE: International Reading Association.

Templeton, S. (2003). Spelling. In J. Flood, D. Lapp, J.R. Squire, & J.M. Jensen (Eds.), *Handbook of research on teaching the English language arts* (2nd ed., pp. 738–751). Mahwah, NJ: Erlbaum.

Templeton, S., Johnston, F., Bear, D., & Invernizzi, M. (2009). *Words their way: Word sorts for derivational relations spellers* (2nd ed.). Boston: Pearson Education.

Thompson, M. (2008). Multimodal teaching and learning: Creating spaces for content teachers. *Journal of Adolescent & Adult Literacy, 52*(2), 144–153. doi:10.1598/JAAL.52.2.5

Tierney, R.J., & Readence, J.E. (2005). *Reading strategies and practices: A compendium* (6th ed.). Boston: Pearson.

Topping, K. (2001). *Peer assisted learning: A practical guide for teachers.* Cambridge, MA: Brookline.

Torgesen, J.K., Rashotte, C.A., & Alexander, A.W. (2001). Principles of fluency instruction in reading: Relationships with established empirical outcomes. In M. Wolf (Ed.), *Dyslexia, fluency, and the brain* (pp. 333–355). Timonium, MD: York.

Tovani, C. (2000). *I read it, but I don't get it: Comprehension strategies for adolescent readers*. Portland, ME: Stenhouse.

Unsworth, L., & Heberle, V. (2009). *Teaching multimodal literacy in English as a foreign language*. Oakville, CT: Brown.

Vacca, R.T., & Vacca, J.L. (2008). *Content area reading: Literacy and learning across the curriculum* (9th ed.). Boston: Pearson/Allyn & Bacon.

Vacca, R.T., Vacca, J.L., & Gove, M.K. (2000). *Reading and learning to read* (4th ed.). New York: Longman.

Vadasy, P.F., & Sanders, E.A. (2008). Repeated reading intervention: Outcomes and interactions with readers' skills and classroom instruction. *Journal of Educational Psychology, 100*(2), 272–290. doi:10.1037/0022-0663.100.2.272

Viise, N.M. (1996). A study of the spelling development of adult literacy learners compared with that of classroom children. *Journal of Literacy Research, 28*(4), 561–587. doi:10.1080/10862969609547940

Webb, N.L. (1999). *Alignment of science and mathematics standards and assessments in four states*. Research Monograph No. 18, published jointly by the National Institute for Science Education and the Council of Chief State School Officers.

Wheelock, A. (1999). Junior Great Books: Reading for meaning in urban schools. *Educational Leadership, 57*(2), 47–50.

White, T.G. (2005). Effects of systematic and strategic analogy-based phonics on grade 2 students' word reading and reading comprehension. *Reading Research Quarterly, 40*(2), 234–255. doi:10.1598/RRQ.40.2.5

Wood, K.D., Lapp, D., Flood, J., & Taylor, D.B. (2008). *Guiding readers through text: Strategy guides for new times* (2nd ed.). Newark, DE: International Reading Association.

Zgonc, Y. (1999). *Phonological awareness: The missing piece to help crack the reading code*. Eau Claire, WI: Otter Creek Institute.

Zigler, E., & Finn-Stevenson, M. (2007). From research to policy and practice: The school of the 21st century. *The American Journal of Orthopsychiatry, 77*(2), 175–181. doi:10.1037/0002-9432.77.2.175

Zwiers, J. (2010). *Building reading comprehension habits in grades 6–12: A toolkit of classroom activities* (2nd ed.). Newark, DE: International Reading Association.

Index

Note. Page numbers followed by *f, t,* or *r* indicate figures, tables, and reproducibles, respectively.

intelligences: multiple, aligned to whole-learner standards, 5, 6t, 7; spatial, 93, 94
interest in learning, 8–9, 9t
International Reading Association, xi, 19
Interpretative Dialogue strategy, 61–62
Interval Sprints strategy, 69
Invernizzi, M., 30, 40
Irvin, J., xi, 8, 11, 20
Irwin, J.W., 85, 136
Istifci, I., 79

J

Jackson, C.J., 7
Jang, H., 8
Jenkins, J.R., 49
Jensen, E., 7, 8, 93, 113
Jewitt, C., 13
Johns, J.L., 48, 67
Johnson, E., 15
Johnston, A.M., 136
Johnston, F., 30, 40
Johnston, P.H., 19
Juel, C., 102

K

Kamil, M.L., 24, 78
Kane, S., 76, 116, 131
Keene, E.O., 119, 121, 129
Kelly, M.J., 118
key element, 140, 141
Kieffer, M.J., 23
Kinniburgh, L., 60
Klauda, S.L., 48
Klausmeier, H.J., 99
Klotz, M.B., 18
Knowledge Rating strategy, 103–104
Kohn, A., 7, 8
Konstantopoulos, S., 15
Kossack, S., 78
Krathwohl, D., 2, 16
Kress, G., 13

Kucan, L., 78
Kunen, S., 16

L

Laberge, M.J., 113
Lam, P., 47
Lapp, D., 112, 113, 123, 132, 134
Laster, B.P., 19
Lavoie, R., 8
learning styles, 7
Lee, C.D., 13
Lenski, S.D., 7, 111
Lenz, B.K., 32
Lesaux, N.K., 23
Leslie, M., 68
level of texts and fluency strategies, 49, 58
Levine, M., 7
Lewis, J., 7, 111
linguistic, definition of, 79, 80
Linnenbrink-Garcia, L., 8
literacy needs of adolescent learners, 7–8
Literary Tours strategy, 75–76
Low-Level Stamina strategy, 70
Loxterman, J.A., 119

M

main idea, 136
Main Idea Wheel strategy, 138, 174r
Manzo, A.V., 30, 131
Manzo, U.C., 30
Marcell, B.T., 65
Martin, G.L., 50
Marzano, R.J., 12, 15, 77
Maslow, A.H., 7
Matthew effect, 14–15
Mayer, R.E., 79
McGinley, W.J., 126
McKeown, M.G., 13, 78, 119
McKnight, M.A., 15
McNamara, D.S., 113
McNaught, C., 47